W9-AAZ-517

EYE ON
Art

MICHELANGELO

by Phyllis Raybin Emert

LUCENT BOOKS
A part of Gale, Cengage Learning

GALE
CENGAGE Learning·

Detroit • New York • San Francisco • New Haven, Conn • Waterville, Maine • London

© 2012 Gale, Cengage Learning

ALL RIGHTS RESERVED. No part of this work covered by the copyright herein may be reproduced, transmitted, stored, or used in any form or by any means graphic, electronic, or mechanical, including but not limited to photocopying, recording, scanning, digitizing, taping, Web distribution, information networks, or information storage and retrieval systems, except as permitted under Section 107 or 108 of the 1976 United States Copyright Act, without the prior written permission of the publisher.

Every effort has been made to trace the owners of copyrighted material.

LIBRARY OF CONGRESS CATALOGING-IN-PUBLICATION DATA

Emert, Phyllis Raybin.
  Michelangelo / by Phyllis Raybin Emert.
    pages cm -- (Eye on art)
  Includes bibliographical references and index.
  ISBN 978-1-4205-0696-9 (hardback)
  1. Michelangelo Buonarroti, 1475-1564--Juvenile literature. 2. Artists--Italy--Biography--Juvenile literature. I. Emert, Phyllis. II. Title.
  N6923.B9E44 2012
  709.2--dc23
  [B]
                                                        2012002752

Lucent Books
27500 Drake Rd.
Farmington Hills, MI 48331

ISBN-13: 978-1-4205-0696-9
ISBN-10: 1-4205-0696-X

Printed in the United States of America
1 2 3 4 5 6 7 16 15 14 13 12

CONTENTS

IN MEMORY OF BLONDIE THE BRAVE

Foreword

"Art has no other purpose than to brush aside . . . everything that veils reality from us in order to bring us face to face with reality itself."

—French philosopher Henri-Louis Bergson

Some thirty-one thousand years ago, early humans painted strikingly sophisticated images of horses, bison, rhinoceroses, bears, and other animals on the walls of a cave in southern France. The meaning of these elaborate pictures is unknown, although some experts speculate that they held ceremonial significance. Regardless of their intended purpose, the Chauvet-Pont-d'Arc cave paintings represent some of the first known expressions of the artistic impulse.

From the Paleolithic era to the present day, human beings have continued to create works of visual art. Artists have developed painting, drawing, sculpture, engraving, and many other techniques to produce visual representations of landscapes, the human form, religious and historical events, and countless other subjects. The artistic impulse also finds expression in glass, jewelry, and new forms inspired by new technology. Indeed, judging by humanity's prolific artistic output throughout history, one must conclude that the compulsion to produce art is an inherent aspect of being human, and the results are among humanity's greatest cultural achievements: masterpieces such as the architectural marvels of ancient Greece, Michelangelo's perfectly rendered statue *David*, Vincent van Gogh's visionary painting *Starry Night*, and endless other treasures.

The creative impulse serves many purposes for society. At its most basic level, art is a form of entertainment or the means for a satisfying or pleasant aesthetic experience. But art's true power lies not in its potential to entertain and delight but in its ability to enlighten, to reveal the truth, and by doing so to uplift the human spirit and transform the human race.

One of the primary functions of art has been to serve religion. For most of Western history, for example, artists were paid by the church to produce works with religious themes and subjects. Art was thus a tool to help human beings transcend mundane, secular reality and achieve spiritual enlightenment. One of the best-known, and largest-scale, examples of Christian religious art is the Sistine Chapel in the Vatican in Rome. In 1508 Pope Julius II commissioned Italian Renaissance artist Michelangelo to paint the chapel's vaulted ceiling, an area of 640 square yards (535 sq. m). Michelangelo spent four years on scaffolding, his neck craned, creating a panoramic fresco of some three hundred human figures. His paintings depict Old Testament prophets and heroes, sibyls of Greek mythology, and nine scenes from the book of Genesis, including the Creation of Adam, the Fall of Adam and Eve from the Garden of Eden, and the Flood. The ceiling of the Sistine Chapel is considered one of the greatest works of Western art and has inspired the awe of countless Christian pilgrims and other religious seekers. As eighteenth-century German poet and author Johann Wolfgang von Goethe wrote, "Until you have seen this Sistine Chapel, you can have no adequate conception of what man is capable of."

In addition to inspiring religious fervor, art can serve as a force for social change. Artists are among the visionaries of any culture. As such, they often perceive injustice and wrongdoing and confront others by reflecting what they see in their work. One classic example of art as social commentary was created in May 1937, during the brutal Spanish civil war. On May 1 Spanish artist Pablo Picasso learned of the recent attack on the small Basque village of Guernica by German airplanes allied with fascist forces led by Francisco Franco. The German pilots had used the village for target practice, a three-hour bombing that killed sixteen hundred civilians. Picasso, living in Paris, channeled his outrage over the massacre into his painting *Guernica,* a black, white, and gray mural that depicts dismembered animals and fractured human figures whose faces are contorted in agonized expressions. Initially, critics and the public condemned the painting as an incoherent hodgepodge, but the work soon came to be seen as a powerful antiwar statement and remains an iconic symbol of the violence and terror that dominated world events during the remainder of the twentieth century.

The impulse to create art—whether painting animals with crude pigments on a cave wall, sculpting a human form from marble, or commemorating human tragedy in a mural—thus serves many purposes. It offers an entertaining diversion, nourishes the imagination and the spirit, decorates and beautifies the world, and chronicles the age. But underlying all these functions is the desire to reveal that which is obscure—to illuminate, clarify, and perhaps ennoble. As Picasso himself stated, "The purpose of art is washing the dust of daily life off our souls."

The Eye on Art series is intended to assist readers in understanding the various roles of art in society. Each volume offers an in-depth exploration of a major artistic movement, medium, figure, or profession. All books in the series are beautifully illustrated with full-color photographs and diagrams. Riveting narrative, clear technical explanation, informative sidebars, fully documented quotes, a bibliography, and a thorough index all provide excellent starting points for research and discussion. With these features, the Eye on Art series is a useful introduction to the world of art—a world that can offer both insight and inspiration.

Introduction

A Life of Troubled Brilliance

Michelangelo was one of the greatest artists of all time and gave the world some of the most magnificent artwork ever created. Recognized as an artistic genius in his own time, he focused on the beauty, movement, and expression of the human body. During his lifetime (1475–1564), both religious and secular society had a high regard for the classical art of ancient Greece and Rome, and this greatly influenced Michelangelo's work during the Italian Renaissance after the Middle Ages.

In the second half of his life, Michelangelo began to embrace Mannerism, an art form that was a reaction to the classical forms of beauty. Whereas the art of the Renaissance embraced grace, harmony, and lifelike subjects, Mannerists focused on unrealistic and exaggerated poses and elongated and twisted limbs. Many of Michelangelo's later major works tended toward Mannerism with a distortion of scale and perspective and agitated body movements of the subjects.

Opinions and attitudes about art changed in the last years of the life of Michelangelo. The Reformation, an attempt to correct the corruption and abuses of the Roman Catholic Church, gave rise to the creation of Protestant churches. The Council of Trent formed the basis of the Counter-Reformation by the Catholics and resulted in the prohibition of the use of nudity in art in 1563. Artwork was now expected to illustrate scenes from the Bible, and a focus on the human body was prohibited. A painting or sculpture was judged on its religious instructional value, not on artistic achievement or beauty. Artwork of the naked human body was considered improper and indecent. These viewpoints resulted in criticism of Michelangelo's works and signaled the end of the Italian Renaissance.

While he was still alive, two major biographies were written about Michelangelo. The first came out in 1550, written by Italian painter and biographer Giorgio Vasari, and focused on Michelangelo as an artist. The second was published in 1553 by Michelangelo's student, Ascanio Condivi. Condivi's biography contains material from Michelangelo himself that had not been included in Vasari's edition. Vasari then published a revised and expanded second edition in 1568, which includes details from Condivi and information about the years leading up to the artist's death in 1564.

Vasari calls him the "greatest artist of his age."[1] Author Jayne Pettit refers to him as the "genius of the Renaissance."[2] Art history professor William E. Wallace, meanwhile, calls him the first "superstar artist."[3] Vasari believed that Michelangelo was a "divinely favored" gift from God. He writes, "The great Ruler of Heaven looked down and . . . resolved . . . to send to earth a genius universal in each art, to show single-handed the perfection of line and shadow." According to Vasari, "He was sent into this world by God to help artists to learn from his life, his character, and his works what a true artist should be."[4]

Michelangelo was a man of many contradictions. He was described as tightfisted and quick-tempered. Yet he was generous with his family and friends. Vasari states, "Although rich he lived like a poor man."[5] Upon his death, a wooden chest under his bed was discovered, filled with gold coins. He supported his dependent relatives, who always bothered him with their financial problems. However, he loved and was devoted to these same people and worked to reestablish and elevate the family name of Buonarroti throughout his life.

Michelangelo in his studio. He has been called the greatest artist of his age and the "genius of the Renaissance."

According to biographers, despite his success Michelangelo was not a happy man. Art conservator and Michelangelo expert Antonio Forcellino in his book *Michelangelo: A Tormented Life* writes, "He trusted no one. . . . He always feared deceit, persecution and fraud," and "he lived like a wretch." Forcellino referred to Michelangelo's life as "miseries, conflicts, and sufferings . . . ordinary in its grimness."[6]

Michelangelo survived social and religious upheavals and a series of European invasions and wars in Italy. He outlived his rivals, many stubborn and controlling popes, and his beloved family and friends. A deeply religious man, he never stopped worrying about death and the salvation of his soul, but he lived to the age of eighty-nine, elderly by even today's standards.

Michelangelo had a rare gift that was fortunately recognized during his early years—first by the painter with whom he apprenticed, Domenico Ghirlandaio, next by the influential and wealthy ruler of Florence, Lorenzo de' Medici, and then by the outstanding patron of the arts and warrior pope, Julius II. These relationships enabled him to create works of beauty such as the *David*, the *Pietà*, the Sistine Chapel ceiling, the *Last Judgment*, and the architecture of St. Peter's Basilica. He was also an outstanding poet, writing sonnets to his friends, family, and acquaintances about art and beauty, faith, love, and death.

When Michelangelo was asked by a friend why he never married and had children, Vasari writes, Michelangelo replied that his many wives were his art, and his numerous works were his children. "And they will live a while however valueless."[7] It was a bit of an understatement. The works of Michelangelo will live forever as priceless masterpieces to be admired, to influence, and to inspire.

1

Early Years: The Developing Artist

The Buonarroti Simoni family was well respected and held many government positions in Florence, Italy. Their ancestors could be traced back several hundred years in the city. When Ludovico di Lionardi di Buonarroti Simoni married Francesca di Neri del Miniato di Sera in 1472, the family had fallen on financial hard times. Their first son, Lionardo, was born in 1473. Then in 1475 Ludovico Buonarroti accepted a six-month position as podesta [magistrate or judge] for two mountain villages, Chiusi and Caprese, outside of Florence. As podesta, Ludovico decided disputes between local farmers and shepherds and was given a stone house in which he and his family lived. His salary and expenses covered several clerks, servants, and a horseman.

Ludovico's second son, Michelangelo, was born on March 6, 1475 at Caprese in the early morning hours. The name Michelangelo, after the archangel Michael who brought souls to judgment, rescued the faithful, and fought against evil, was an uncommon one at the time. The village of Chiusi had a church dedicated to the Archangel Michael, and it is possible that Ludovico named his second son to honor the village and the church. Ascanio Condivi writes in *The Life of Michelangelo* that Mercury and Venus were in the house ruled by Jupiter at the time of the great artist's birth, and this foretold "that the birth should be of a noble and high genius, able to succeed in every undertaking, but principally in those arts that delight the senses, such as painting, sculpture, and architecture."[8]

Early Experiences

Ludivico's term of office was up a month after Michelangelo was born, so the Buonarrotis went back to the small farm that Ludovico had inherited from his father in Settignano, three miles from Florence. There they dropped the baby off with a wet nurse, who was a woman hired to feed and care for the child in infancy. This arrangement was customary in Florence for upper-class families, and the child was returned to the household once it reached the age of about two or three.

Michelangelo was born in this house on March 6, 1475 in Caprese, Italy.

The wet nurse was the daughter of a stonecutter and also married to one. Michelangelo used to joke later in life that being a sculptor was passed down to him through the milk of his wet nurse, and that is why he loved working with stone. He told Giorgio Vasari that he had "sucked in chisels and hammers with my nurse's milk."[9]

Family Ties

Michelangelo and his older brother, Lionardo, were soon joined by three additional brothers. His mother, Francesca, gave birth to Buonarroto in 1477, Giovansimone in 1479, and Gismondo in 1481. That same year, twenty-five-year-old Francesca died, possibly from complications of childbirth. The brothers were 8, 6, 4, 2, and in infancy when they lost their mother. Four years later, when Michelangelo was ten, his father remarried Lucrezia degli Ubaldeini da Gagliano.

Author and journalist George Bull describes Michelangelo as an "alert, sensitive, intelligent, introspective and quick-tempered boy, prone to sickness, but resilient, with black hair and brown eyes flecked with yellow."[10] Some art historians, such as Antonio Forcellino, believe the lack of female tenderness and motherly warmth caused him to be fearful of women and develop an inner emptiness. On the other hand, William E. Wallace in *Michelangelo: The Artist, The Man, and His Times* notes that "Michelangelo displays a profound sensitivity to feminine beauty and a special tenderness for Christ's mother, who is one of the most frequent figures in his art. Themes of maternal love, loss, and separation abound in Michelangelo's art and poetry."[11]

As for his father, author Ross King in *Michelangelo & the Pope's Ceiling* writes, "Michelangelo inherited little from his father except hypochondria, self-pity and a snobbish conviction that the Buonarroti were descended from a noble and ancient family."[12] Ludovico sent his son to receive formal schooling, but Michelangelo's main interest was in drawing and painting, not in academics. He used every spare moment to draw pictures of local buildings, churches, and particular sculptures and paintings in Florence.

PIETRO TORRIGIANI AND MICHELANGELO'S NOSE

Michelangelo was confident in his abilities as a young artist, although some might have called him a bit arrogant. He worked hard and enjoyed the admiration of the other artists. In addition to sculpture, he drew copies of paintings and artwork in the San Marcos garden. In particular, Michelangelo admired the work of the great Italian painter Masaccio. Pietro Torrigiani was another talented young artist who worked in San Marcos and related the following story of Michelangelo to fellow artist Benvenuto Cellini, which was printed in his *Memoirs of Cellini,* written in the mid-1500s but not published until 1728.

> Buonarroti and I used, when we were boys, to go into the Church of the Carmine to learn drawing from the Chapel of Masaccio. It was Buonarroti's habit to banter all who were drawing there, and one day, when he was annoying me, I got more angry than usual, and clenching my fist, I gave him such a blow on the nose that I felt bone and cartilage go down like biscuit beneath my knuckles; and this mark of mine he will carry with him to his grave.[1]

Michelangelo biographer Ascanio Condivi writes about the same incident in *The Life of Michelangelo:* "When he was a boy, one Torrigiano [Pietro] de' Torrigiani, a brutal and proud fellow; with a blow almost broke the cartilage, so that Michael Angelo was carried home as one dead; for this Torrigiani was banished from Florence, and he came to a bad end."[2]

Whether Torrigiani really was banished from Florence is not known, but he did leave for Rome sometime after this incident. Much of his career was spent in England and Spain and he was reputed to have had a violent temper by some historians. Michelangelo's flattened and most likely broken nose never healed properly. His face, which was not particularly handsome to begin with, was forever marked by his conspicuously flat and somewhat crooked nose.

1. Quoted in John T. Spike. *Young Michelangelo: The Path to the Sistine.* New York: Vendome, 2010, p. 45.
2. Ascanio Condivi. *The Life of Michelangelo.* Translated by C.B. Holroyd. London: Pallas Athene, 2006, p. 172.

A Little Help from a Friend

One of Michelangelo's friends, Francesco Granacci, an older painting student, urged him to study art and loaned him drawings so he could practice and learn from them. Michelangelo began to accompany Granacci to the workshop of Domenico Ghirlandaio and his brothers, who were accomplished and well-known painters in Florence.

When his son decided to become an artist, Ludovico became angry. He believed that art was not an acceptable occupation for a gentleman to pursue because painters were merely craftsmen who worked with their hands. Ascanio Condivi writes, "His father and his uncles, who held the art in contempt, were much displeased, and often beat him severely for it; They were so ignorant of the excellence and nobility of art that they thought shame to have her in the house. This, although it made him very unhappy, was not enough to turn him back, but, on the contrary, made him more bold."[13]

Eventually Ludovico relented, and Michelangelo was sent to be an apprentice in the workshop of Ghirlandaio. He joined his friend Granacci and other young men in learning art and painting. In return, Ghirlandaio agreed to give thirteen-year-old Michelangelo a salary of six florins the first year, eight the second year, and ten the third year.

Forcellino believes that Ludovico enrolled his son into Ghirlandaio's workshop because the family needed the money. These financial difficulties led Ludivico to believe that Michelangelo would never be part of the upper classes, but a member of the artisan and working class.

At the Workshop

Ghirlandaio was a well-established painter of murals when Michelangelo came to his workshop in Florence. Young aspiring artists were taught design and coloring techniques, drawing with pen and brush, and fresco painting from books, live models, and on-the-job experience. According to Forcellino, "The apprentice had to learn to look after the tools of the trade and keep them in complete working order. Then he had to become familiar with the materials . . . [and start to assist in] preparing the surfaces for painting, spreading the glue and chalk primer over wooden surfaces . . . and painting in small portions of the background."[14]

Michelangelo used all of his spare time to practice his drawing by copying models in the workshop and works of great artists of the past. In many cases, Michelangelo drew the copy so well that others could not tell which was the original and which was the copy. Using smoke, he could even make them look timeworn. Soon the young artist surpassed the other students and equaled and occasionally surpassed the teacher's works. Ghirlandaio commented to Giorgio Vasari that Michelangelo knew more than he did.

Forcellino writes that Ghirlandaio may have been envious and disapproving of his arrogant but talented young pupil. So when Florentine ruler Lorenzo de' Medici asked him to send the best of his students to his San Marco garden, Ghirlandaio was happy to recommend Michelangelo and his friend Granacci. History is unclear about when Michelangelo made this move, but it was sometime between the age of fourteen and sixteen. In the famous and beautiful Medici garden, Michelangelo turned his attention to sculpture. He preferred the reality of the three-dimensional shape over the flat, one-dimensional surface of a painting or fresco. Ludovico was even more upset that his second son wanted to become a sculptor, which he considered to be a glorified stonecutter, but Michelangelo's mind was made up.

The Magnificent Medici Gardens

The Medici garden of San Marco, adjacent to the large Medici family estate (palazzo) was filled with trees, flowers, and Lorenzo's collection of ancient and modern statues, frescoes, paintings, and drawings. The garden was surrounded by high walls, and there was a house and sleeping quarters on the property. Young, talented artists were invited to the garden to study, copy, and create artwork under the supervision of well-known sculptor Bertoldo di Giovanni.

One of the first jobs Michelangelo had was creating sculptures for the Medici garden in Florence.

Among Michelangelo's first projects was to reproduce the head of a faun in marble. Lorenzo praised the workmanship and technique of the piece, but he joked to the fifteen-year-old that the faun was very old and should be missing some of its teeth. After Lorenzo left, Michelangelo chiseled away a few of the teeth. When the Prince of Florence returned, he was impressed by the seriousness of the young artist and the beauty of the finished work.

Earliest Works at San Marco

In addition to the *Head of a Faun*, Michelangelo sculpted the *Madonna of the Stairs* in low-relief at age sixteen, and the

Battle of the Centaurs in high-relief at age seventeen while working at the Medici garden. A relief sculpture is a design that projects out from the surface of the stone to varying degrees.

The *Madonna of the Stairs* is a small stone carving that measures 26 x 18 inches (66 x 45.7cm) in size with only 2 inches (5.1cm) of relief projection. Mary, in profile, is seated in the foreground and takes up the entire space. On her lap, she feeds the Christ child (or he is asleep) with his back to the viewer and his face hidden from sight. Mary gazes off in the distance as she lifts her cloak to shelter the child. There are smaller, shallower figures of children on the steps and a railing behind the dominant figure of Mary.

Another of his early sculptures, called *Battle of the Centaurs,* Michelangelo decided to carve after hearing the story of the mythological battle. Bull describes the work: "The small, highly polished but unfinished relief shows part of a melee [brawl] of athletic male nudes linked in close embrace, with set faces and sensually expressive bodies."[15] Art historian John T. Spike in his book *Young Michelangelo: The Path to the Sistine* states that the figures in the *Battle of the Centaurs* "appear to emerge from the underlying marble."[16] Art history professor James Beck in his book *Three Worlds of Michelangelo* declares that Michelangelo's *Battle* reveals "enormous creative potential. These figures, 10 or 12 inches (25.4 or 30.48cm) high, would soon enough burst forth, expand twenty-fold, and evolve into massive three-dimensional creatures."[17] In *Battle of the Centaurs* Michelangelo concentrated on the naked human body engaged in vigorous activity, a theme that would become the focus of his future work.

Lorenzo believed Michelangelo was destined for greatness and talked to Ludovico about his plan to invite Michelangelo to reside with his family in the Medici palazzo. Ludovico agreed, and Michelangelo moved in with the Medicis. Lorenzo eventually was able to get Ludovico a simple public service job in the customs house in Florence.

Life with the Medicis

According to Condivi, Lorenzo

> gave Michael Angelo a good room in his own house with all that he needed, treating him like a son, with a seat at his table, which, as of such a man, was frequented every day by noblemen and men of great affairs . . . by all of them Michael Angelo was caressed and incited to his honourable work; but above all by the Magnificent, who would often call for him many times in the day to show him gems . . . medals, and such like things of great price, seeing that he had genius and good judgment.[18]

Michelangelo lived with Lorenzo's three sons, Piero, Giovanni, and Giuliano, his nephew Giulio, and four daughters, as well as an array of philosophers, poets, and scholars who were frequent visitors. Lorenzo groomed Piero to take over the family banking business and the governing of the city. He managed to secretly obtain the position of cardinal from the church for his second son, Giovanni, when he was only thirteen years old. Giovanni went on to become Pope Leo X, and Lorenzo's nephew Giulio, the illegitimate son of his deceased brother, went on to become Pope Clement VII. Lorenzo also made good matches for his daughters to provide for the continuation of Medici power.

Lorenzo maintained power and control in Florence because he eliminated his wealthy adversaries and strengthened his allies among the lower and middle classes. More important, he administered justice impartially and respected traditions of Florence that brought honor and integrity to the city. He was a patron who promoted beautiful works of art and architecture throughout the city.

Death and Upheaval

Lorenzo de' Medici fell ill suddenly and died on April 8, 1492, at the age of forty-three. Florence had lost a diplomat and statesman who had maintained peace among the various

FLORENCE AND THE MEDICIS

The city of Florence, a leader of the Italian Renaissance, was a flourishing city-state with a population of about sixty thousand people. The Humanist movement influenced early Florentine government, focusing on the individual power of man to shape future events. This was in contrast to the earlier Middle Ages when church doctrine and fate dominated, the arts were considered blasphemous, and education was limited to clergymen. Humanism promoted and encouraged the arts and education for people other than members of the church. Representatives of the wealthy merchant guilds ruled the city and discussed and voted on important issues. Art history professor James Beck in *Three Worlds of Michelangelo* notes that the citizens of Florence were proud of their seven blessings—"full liberty, rich and well-dressed people; a river, . . . a government . . . ; a university; . . . guilds representing the diverse arts; and . . . banks that provided services for the entire world."

The Medicis were prosperous and well-known figures because of the successful Medici Bank, which had branches all throughout Europe. The bank played a significant role in trade and commerce, and the family's accumulated wealth led to political power. Lorenzo de' Medici, like his grandfather, Cosimo, and father, Piero, before him, amassed great wealth, power, and patronage, and he was determined to continue the Medici family dominance. Under Lorenzo's leadership, Florence blossomed as the center of Renaissance art and learning. The city was the home of the Plato Academy, where scholars discussed philosophy and the classics, religious plays were staged, and festivals were held throughout the area. There were jousting tournaments, dances, fencing competitions, and even a horse race to celebrate the feast day of St. John.

James Beck. *Three Worlds of Michelangelo.* New York: W.W. Norton, 1999, pp. 78–79.

city-states of Italy for many years. Michelangelo had lost a friend, a mentor, and a patron. Michelangelo returned to his father's home to grieve, and Piero de' Medici became the ruler of Florence and the head of the Medici family.

At home, Michelangelo learned that his older brother, Lionardo, had entered a monastery to become a monk. The family's financial situation was poor, and Ludovico hoped that Michelangelo could get some paid commissions from a new patron. At first, Michelangelo was very depressed and devastated about the death of Lorenzo. Once his grief had passed, he decided to learn all he could about human anatomy to help him be a better sculptor.

Studying Anatomy

Since Michelangelo wanted his human figures to appear as realistic and alive as possible, it seemed logical for him to study them firsthand by dissecting human corpses before burial. Although the Church was hesitant about allowing dissection, the skill and talent of the young artist convinced the prior of the church of Santo Spirito to allow Michelangelo appropriate space and subjects for detailed study. Michelangelo made many anatomical drawings that helped him in his understanding of the muscles, bones, and tissues involved in human movement. In return for the kindness shown to him by the prior of Santo Spirito, sometime around 1493 or 1494 Michelangelo made him a wooden crucifix, 4 feet 5 inches x 4 feet 5 inches (1.35 x 1.35m), slightly smaller than life-size, for the high altar of the church.

Condivi writes that Michelangelo "gave up dissection because it turned his stomach so that he could neither eat nor drink with benefit . . . [but] he did not give up until he was so learned and rich in such knowledge that he often had in his mind the wish to write, for the sake of sculptors and painters, a treatise on the movements of the human body."[19]

After finishing his anatomical studies, Michelangelo bought a large, weathered block of stone, and in about 1493

THE MASTER AT THIRTEEN: MICHELANGELO'S FIRST PAINTING?

The small painting was first offered for auction and catalogued as "from the workshop of Domenico Ghirlandaio." It was a reproduction of an engraving by Martin Schongauer called "The Torment of St. Anthony" dated about 1488. Carol Vogel of the *New York Times* describes it as "an oil and tempera on a wooden panel, depicting the saint poised in midair and beaten by demons." Both Michelangelo biographers, Giorgio Vasari and Ascanio Condivi, note the Schongauer painting in their writings.

Vogel describes the 18.50 inch x 13.25 inch (47cm x 33.7cm) painting as "at least one-third larger than the engraving. It is also not an exact copy; Michelangelo took liberties," she states. "He depicted St. Anthony holding his head more erect and with an expression more detached than sad," writes Vogel. "He also added a landscape to the bottom of the composition, and created monsters that are more dramatic than those in the engraving."

Art scholars still disagree as to whether it was painted by Michelangelo. After detailed examination and cleaning, Keith Christiansen of the Metropolitan Museum of Art in New York said it was absolutely painted by Michelangelo.

So did Evan McCauley Lee, director of the Kimbell Art Museum in Fort Worth, Texas, which purchased the painting in 2009. However, Michael Hirst, a British scholar of Michelangelo, said it was not painted by the master. Time will tell whether there will ever be agreement among the art scholars.

Carol Vogel, "By the Hand of a Very Young Master?" *New York Times*, May 13, 2009, www.nytimes.com/2009/05/13/arts/design/13pain.html.

Michelangelo's first painting is thought to be The Torment of St. Anthony, *painted in 1488. Art historians believe Michelangelo worked on the piece.*

Piero de' Medici was only twenty years old when he assumed the position of his late father. He lacked his father's leadership, wisdom, and diplomatic skills, and the citizenry rose up against him.

made a statue of the Greek hero Hercules, son of Zeus, who was well-known for his immense strength. The statue was 7 feet 7 ½ inches (2.33m) tall. It was purchased by the wealthy Strozzi family in Florence. Eventually, the *Hercules* made its way to the court of the king of France, and then historians lost track of it.

Piero de' Medici Not His Father's Son

Condivi writes of a big snowstorm in Florence while Michelangelo was living with Ludovico. Piero sent for the young artist to carve a snow statue in the palazzo courtyard. Michelangelo created another Hercules out of snow and ice that did not thaw for a week, so many Florentines were able to view and admire the piece. Forcellino notes that Piero was not the visionary his father had been. "Piero's frivolous mind was incapable of conceiving anything more lasting than a snow sculpture."[20] Piero was so pleased he asked Michelangelo to move back to the Medici palace, and Michelangelo accepted his invitation.

Meanwhile, the state of affairs in Florence was getting worse. Piero de' Medici was only twenty years old when he assumed the position of his late father, and he lacked the wisdom, diplomacy, and grace of Lorenzo. Piero's lack of leadership, childish ways, and abuse of power made him unpopular with the people. Florence ended up in the middle of a dispute with Charles VIII of France, when Charles marched into Italy in 1494 to claim the city-state of Naples. The French attacked Florentine towns on the way to Naples, and Piero, on his own, went to negotiate with the French king without informing the city government. Piero ended up giving in to French demands. He allowed the French to pass through Florence, and the city rose up against Piero.

Michelangelo fled from Florence in 1494 without telling anybody. He believed the people would associate him with the Medicis, and he felt in danger there. Piero and his followers also escaped from the city, and the Dominican friar Girolamo Savonarola (1452–1498) took control. Savonarola had an extremely conservative view of religion, and many were alarmed at his intolerant view of the arts.

After a few days in Venice, Michelangelo and several companions traveled to Bologna. Low on funds, he stayed there for a year to earn money. Piero had also fled to Bologna, and it is believed that both were in the city at the same time. Michelangelo obtained several commissions for artwork and eventually made his way to the city of Rome.

2

The Young Genius in Rome and Florence

According to Ascanio Condivi, a law in Bologna required visitors to get a seal of red wax on their thumbnail before entering the city. Michelangelo and his companions mistakenly passed through the city gates without getting sealed. The young artist was immediately taken into custody by local security forces and fined fifty lire. Since he had no money to pay the fine, Michelangelo remained in detention. One of the wealthy governors of Bologna, Gianfrancesco Aldovrandi, upon learning Michelangelo was a sculptor and had connections with the Medicis, secured his release and invited him to live free of charge at his home.

The Bologna governor offered him a city commission of thirty ducats to work on several small statues for the tomb of St. Dominic in the Church of San Domenico. These early works included *Angel Bearing a Candlestick*, also called *Candelabrum Angel*, 20¼ inches (51.4cm) high, and figures of St. Petronius and St. Procolo, 25¼ inches (64.1cm) high and 23 inches (58.4cm) high, respectively.

Once things had settled down in Florence, Michelangelo went home for a few months and carved two new pieces, a young John the Baptist, commissioned by Lorenzo

Bologna's Gianfrancesco Aldovrandi secured Michelangelo's release from detention and hired him. Michelangelo worked on many small statues, among them the *Candelabrum Angel* for the tomb of St. Dominic in the Church of San Domenico in Bologna.

di Pierfrancesco (a distant relation of the Medicis), and the *Sleeping Cupid*. The marble cupid was the size of a six-year-old-child lying fast asleep.

The *Sleeping Cupid* Incident

Historians disagree whether the following actually happened, but Michelangelo's friend Lorenzo supposedly suggested that he could sell the *Sleeping Cupid* in Rome for a lot more money if he could make it look like an antique that had been buried in the earth. Michelangelo made the sculpture appear older, and

Lorenzo gave it to a merchant friend in Rome who sold it to the cardinal of San Giorgio, Raffaele Riario, for two hundred ducats. The merchant pocketed most of the money and gave Michelangelo thirty ducats.

When the cardinal found out that the *Sleeping Cupid* had been made in Florence and was not really an antique, he became very angry. After an investigation, Michelangelo was tracked down as the sculptor. Scholars differ as to whether Michelangelo left immediately for Rome to make things right or the cardinal invited him to Rome, but the result was the same. The cardinal got his money back for the *Cupid*, Michelangelo kept the thirty ducats he had originally received, the cardinal became a supporter of the twenty-one-year-old sculptor, and Michelangelo stayed in Rome.

His First Large Sculpture— Bacchus

Riario had a personal collection of classical statues, as did many Roman noblemen at that time. He bought a large block of marble for Michelangelo and commissioned him to do a life-size figure. This became the statue of *Bacchus* (5 feet ½ inch [1.84m] high,) for which the young sculptor was paid a total of 150 ducats. John T. Spike writes that this amount "represented what his father would have earned in six years in the customs job he had obtained from Lorenzo de' Medici."[21]

Ascanio Condivi describes the completed *Bacchus*: "This work in form and bearing in every part corresponds to the description of the ancient writers—his aspect, merry; the eyes, squinting and lascivious, like those of people excessively given to the love of wine. He holds a cup in his right hand, like one about to drink, and looks at it lovingly, taking pleasure in the liquor of which he was the inventor."[22] Giorgio Vasari notes the androgynous nature of the statue, "blending in the limbs of the slenderness of a youth and the fleshy roundness of a woman."[23]

According to Spike, the cardinal was not pleased with the statue and considered it inappropriate for a man of the church, since it portrayed excessive drunkenness and lechery.

Cardinal Riario bought a large block of marble and commissioned Michelangelo to do a life-size figure. The result was his *Bacchus*. Michelangelo was paid 150 ducats, but the cardinal found the sculpture inappropriate because it portrayed excessive drunkenness and lechery.

Michelangelo had carved the *Bacchus* at the home of Riario's wealthy banker, Iacopo Gallo. The cardinal never took delivery of the statue, and presumably Gallo purchased the piece for himself and kept it at his home.

Gallo was impressed by the talented Michelangelo and became his patron. He commissioned the young sculptor to carve a beautiful life-size cupid (also known as *Apollo*) of white Carrara marble, holding a bow and arrows. Months later, Gallo recommended Michelangelo to the French cardinal Jean de Bilheres-Lagraulas, who wanted a sculpture to decorate his tomb in St. Peter's.

The First Masterpiece— the *Pietà*

Michelangelo received an advance payment from the cardinal to travel to Carrara to obtain the finest block of white marble. It measured at least 6 feet x 6 feet x 4 feet (1.83m x 1.83m x 1.22m). The entire round-trip journey, including time spent picking out the block, cutting it, and transporting it by cart and then by sea back to Rome, took over six months.

Spike quotes some of the terms in the original contract, dated August 27, 1498:

> Maestro Michelangelo, statuary of Florence . . . shall at his own proper costs make a pieta of marble, that is to say a draped figure of the Virgin Mary, with the dead Christ in her arms, the figures being life-size, for the sum of four hundred and fifty gold ducats in papal gold, to be finished within the term of one year from the beginning of the work. . . . I, Iacopo Gallo, do promise the Most Reverend Monsignore, that the said Michelangelo shall complete said work within one year and that it shall be more beautiful than any work in marble to be seen in Rome today, and such that no master of our own time shall be able to produce a better.[24]

Michelangelo fulfilled all but one part of the agreement. It took him two years and not one to complete the statue because he took many months to carefully polish the marble. Condivi briefly describes the completed *Pietà*: "The Madonna is seated on the stone upon which the Cross was erected, with her dead son on her lap, of so great and so rare a beauty, that no one beholds it but is moved to pity."[25]

Michelangelo's first masterpiece was his sculpture *Pietà*. Condivi described it as "so great and so rare a beauty, that no one beholds it but is moved to pity."

Widespread Fame and a Bit of Criticism

The *Pietà*, finished in 1500, made the twenty-five-year-old Michelangelo famous, with a reputation for creating beautiful works of art. However, some critics complained that the Madonna looked too young in contrast with her Son. Michelangelo explained to Condivi why he made Mary so youthful. He declared that chaste women kept their looks and youth longer than unchaste women. In addition, God wanted to prove her virginity and perpetual purity.

Professor of art history Joachim Poeschke in his book *Michelangelo and His Work: Sculpture of the Italian Renais-*

sance analyzes the *Pietà*, which is 5 feet 8 ½ inches (1.74m) high. "The nude Christ is almost completely framed by the outline of the wide, flowing robe of Mary," writes Poeschke. Michelangelo "managed to balance the vertical orientation of the one figure and the horizontal, or diagonal, line of the other by placing Mary's right foot higher than her left and creating long curving folds below the body of her son. Mary is presenting his corpse to the viewer, inviting us to gaze upon him with the gesture of her left hand."[26] Poeschke notes that the positioning of the figures shows the contrast between life, death, grief and beauty.

CORRESPONDENCE

The writings of Michelangelo provide an insight into the heart and mind of the artist—his opinions on art, beauty, family, love, religion, death, and work at various times of his life. Nearly half of his letters were written to members of his family and offered advice, criticisms, and complaints on everyday matters.

In a letter to his father in Florence, dated August 19, 1497, Michelangelo in Rome writes:

> [Buonarroto] tells me that the merchant, Consiglio, is giving you a lot of trouble, that he won't come to any agreement, and that he wants to have you arrested. I advise you to come to an agreement and pay him a few ducats on account; and whatever you agree to give him, let me know, and I'll send it to you, if you don't have it. Although I have very little money, as I've told you, I'll contrive to borrow it. . . . Don't be surprised if sometimes I have written so irritably. Often I get wrought up by the sort of things that happen to people away from home. Whatever you ask of me, I will send you, even if I have to sell myself as a slave.

Quoted in John T. Spike. *Young Michelangelo: The Path to the Sistine*. New York: Vendome, 2010, p. 106.

The *Pietà* is the only sculpture by Michelangelo that he signed. Vasari relates a story that visitors gazing at the *Pietà* credited another artist as the sculptor. This supposedly angered Michelangelo so much that he carved his name on the sash across Mary's chest. William E. Wallace declares, "The Pieta is a miracle of marble carving: Michelangelo transformed hard rock into soft flesh and drapery, creating a . . . two-figure sculpture group of great dignity and breathtaking beauty."[27]

Homeward Bound

In his letters to his father, Michelangelo pleaded poverty when questioned about money. Michelangelo's favorite brother, Buonarroto Buonarroti, had visited him in 1500 in Rome and found his standard of living to be very poor. The well-known sculptor paid only one and a half ducats a month for his lodgings and slept and ate very little. Yet, according to Spike, by 1500 Michelangelo's bank account "already contained more money than his father earned in ten years,"[28]

Ludovico wrote to his son warning him about his health and asked him to come home to Florence. "Economy is good, but above all things, do not deprive yourself of basic necessities. . . . Take care of your head: keep it moderately warm and never bathe yourself. Keep yourself clean but don't wash yourself. . . . Once again I remind you to devise a way to return as soon as you can: and believe me that when you are here you will have much to do."[29] By this time, the Buonarrotis were looking to Michelangelo as the main financial support of the family and had minimal interest in his artwork.

In 1501 Michelangelo accepted a commission from Cardinal Francesco Todeschini-Piccolomini, who later became Pope Pius III, to carve fifteen small figures for the family altar in the cathedral at Siena. Since he was required to get measurements at Siena and then obtain marble at Carrara, Michelangelo decided to return to Florence after five years in Rome and work on the figures at home. He never finished this commission and became preoccupied by other projects in Florence. Most of the figures were eventually carved by other sculptors.

Michelangelo completed only four of the fifteen statues—St. Peter (4 feet ¾ inches [1.23m] high), St. Paul (4 feet 2 inches (1.27m) high, and St. Gregory and St. Pius, (both 4 feet 5 ⅛ inches [1.35m] high). After his death Michelangelo's sole heir and nephew, Leonardo, returned the advance money to the Piccolomini heirs according to his uncle's wishes.

The Giant Block of Marble

The now-famous sculptor was welcomed back to the Republic of Florence with open arms and kept busy with many private commissions and a particularly large public one. A huge block of marble had been purchased thirty-five years before for a statue of the biblical king David for the Cathedral of Florence. Several sculptors had begun to carve the stone but were unsuccessful, and the block was put aside in the courtyard, neglected

Michelangelo's masterpiece *David* was carved from a single block of marble and stands nearly 17 feet (5.18m) tall. Michelangelo had studied ancient Greek sculptures, and this is evident in the stunning anatomical detail of the work.

and weathered over time. Michelangelo signed a contract with the Guild of Wool Merchants, who maintained the cathedral, to carve the Giant, as the *David* was called, and he worked on it from 1501 to 1504.

Curator of sculpture at the Uffizi Gallery in Florence Umberto Baldini calls the *David* the turning pointing point in Michelangelo's career. "All the positive values that he had gathered in observing the antique and practicing it," writes Baldini, "all his exercises and direct studies on the human body, all the internal spiritual forces that he had thrown into interpreting the world both in myth and reality: all come into play [in the *David*]."[30]

According to Wallace, a laser scanner measured the *David* at nearly 17 feet (5.18m) high. During his work, Michelangelo had a wooden shed put up to shield himself and the marble block from public view. When it was completed, a commission of the best artists in Florence, including Leonardo da Vinci, was appointed to decide where the work should be placed. It was decided that the entrance to the Palazzo Vecchio near the center of government was an appropriate spot. Moving the giant statue, which weighed 6 tons (5.44t), required a sling-like device to keep it safe and suspended off the ground.

The *David* was considered to be a symbol of the city and its republican government—the underdog, threatened by powerful enemies and tyrants, that ultimately vanquished its foes. Some Medici supporters and those who were offended by the statue's nudity protested and threw stones. For the most part, it was widely accepted, praised as a great masterpiece, and imitated by other artists at the time.

Details of *David*

Poeschke writes that the *David*'s "athletically developed torso, like its colossal size and nudity, is a direct borrowing from classical sculpture."[31] Michelangelo carved the statue out of the giant block of marble without adding any other pieces. "It was so exactly to size," writes Condivi, "that the old surface of the outsides of the marble may be seen on the top of the head and

A NOSY OFFICIAL

Michelangelo biographer Giorgio Vasari writes in *The Life of Michelangelo* that Piero Soderini, head of the Florentine government, came to see the statue of David before it was unveiled to the public. The gifted sculptor was doing a bit of retouching to the marble when Soderini remarked that the nose was too large. Instead of being angry or insulted, Michelangelo climbed the framework around the statue and using his chisel, he appeared to (but did not) make a change in the nose, causing a bit of marble dust to fall to the ground below. Then he said to Soderini, "Look now," and the Florentine ruler replied, "I like it better. You have given it life."

Quoted in Giorgio Vasari. *The Life of Michelangelo.* London: Pallas Athene, 2006, p. 59. (First published in Florence in 1550, this translation is based on the expanded second edition of 1568.)

Florence's ruler, Piero Soderini, remarked to Michelangelo that David's nose was too large. The artist then fooled Soderini into thinking he had reduced the nose when he had merely acted like he did. Soderini thought it added life to the statue but not a thing was changed.

in the base."[32] Vasari writes, "The legs are finely turned, the slender flanks divine, and the graceful pose unequalled, while such feet, hands, and head have never been excelled. After seeing this no one need wish to look at any other sculpture or the work of any other artist."[33]

"David stands with his weight shifted to his right leg, suggesting his imminent movement," states Wallace. "The massive torso bends in the opposite direction from his piercing glance. . . . The thick neck and prominent bulging muscles increase the sense of taut preparedness, of a figure ready to unleash coiled energy."[34] Antonio Forcellino calls the *David* "the new god of male beauty."[35]

Other Works in Florence

While Michelangelo was in Florence, he accepted many private commissions in addition to the *David*. The Guild of Wool Merchants wanted him to carve full-size sculptures of the twelve apostles for the cathedral. However, he had too many other commissions and only carved a half-completed statue of St. Matthew in 1506. The contract was annulled, and other sculptors completed the remaining apostles. The *St. Matthew* was about 7 feet (2.13m) tall and was a perfect example of the figure freeing itself from the block of marble with the aid of the sculptor. Only the front part of the *St. Matthew* had been carved, showing a powerfully muscled chest and a twisted, moving body emerging out of the stone.

Piero Soderini, the head of the government in Florence, asked Michelangelo to cast a bronze statue of the *David*, which, when completed, was sent to a collector in France, where it was ultimately lost. Then, a wealthy family of Flemish merchants commissioned him to carve the *Madonna of Bruges* (4 feet 2⅜ inches [1.28m] high). The completed piece was sent to the Church of Notre Dame in Bruges and contributed to Michelangelo's fame and status in northern Europe. Wallace notes that as Michelangelo had done with the *Pieta*, so here also he transformed the marble "into malleable flesh and large, supple folds of drapery."[36]

Michelangelo never finished his *St. Matthew* sculpture. The figure seems to be freeing itself, or emerging, from a block of stone.

Rivalry with Leonardo

When Michelangelo returned to Florence in 1501, the talk of the town was not about the gifted young sculpture's arrival. Instead, Florentines were buzzing about the return of the great master Leonardo da Vinci, who, at nearly fifty, was almost twice Michelangelo's age. In 1503 Da Vinci was commissioned

Aristotile da Sangallo copied parts of Michelangelo's *Battle of Cascina* cartoon for this drawing. Michelangelo's work was studied, handled, and copied by so many artists that it eventually fell to pieces.

to do a fresco in the government council chamber at the Palazzo Vecchio. *The Battle of Anghiari* by Leonardo focuses on the fight over the flag by the cavalry on horseback. However, he never finished the fresco and left Florence for other well-paid commissions in Milan.

In 1504 Michelangelo was assigned to paint *The Battle of Cascina* on the opposite wall of Leonardo's fresco. Michelangelo's painting was supposed to capture the surprise attack of enemy troops from Pisa on Florentine foot soldiers bathing and relaxing in the river. Michelangelo finished the full-size preliminary drawing, or cartoon, (about 1,250 square feet (116.13 sq. m) in size), but never completed the fresco because he was called to Rome by Pope Julius II. If both Leonardo and Michelangelo had finished the painting phase of their commissions, they might have worked together under the same roof in what James Beck states "would have been the most spectacular artistic confrontation of the Renaissance."[37]

The Battle of Cascina

Other artists were so impressed by the figures in the *Battle of Cascina* cartoon that they studied all aspects of the drawing at

Michelangelo was devoted to the arts and loved knowledge to the point that he enjoyed being alone so he could read and learn. Biographer Ascanio Condivi in *The Life of Michelangelo* wrote in 1553 that "by some he was held to be proud, and by others odd and eccentric."[1] He took pleasure in conversing with learned friends, delighted in reading Dante and Petrarch, and studied the Old and New Testament. He loved the human body in a platonic sense, that of spiritual rather than physical love. "No evil thoughts were born in him," states Condivi. "He loved not only human beauty, but universally every beautiful thing."[2]

"All through his life Michael Angelo has been very abstemious [self-denying], taking food more from necessity than from pleasure, especially when at work, at which time, for the most part, he has been content with a piece of bread, which he munched whilst he labored," Condivi writes. "And as he took little food so he took little sleep, which, as he says, rarely did him any good, for sleeping almost always made his head ache, and too much sleep made his stomach bad." Condivi continues, "When he was more robust he often slept in his clothes and with his buskins [laced boots] on; . . . he has sometimes been so long without taking them off that when he did so the skin came off with them like the slough of a snake."[3]

When Michelangelo was involved in a major art project, he focused on what needed to be accomplished so that personal hygiene was often-times overlooked. He may have been insecure about his looks but was very confident in his talent and genius. He liked fame but preferred his privacy. He did not enjoy receiving letters from his family in the middle of a project and complained, "I have written you several times that every time I have a letter of yours I get a headache." Another time, he declared, "Don't write me anymore, because you keep me from working."[4]

1. Ascanio Condivi. *The Life of Michelangelo.* Trans. C.B. Holroyd. London: Pallas Athene, 2006, p. 161.
2. Condivi. *The Life of Michelangelo,* p. 167.
3. Condivi. *The Life of Michelangelo,* pp. 167–168.
4. Quoted in Jayne Pettit. *Michelangelo: Genius of the Renaissance.* New York: Franklin Watts, 1998, p. 39.

length, hoping to learn from it. According to Vasari, Michelangelo

> filled it with nude figures bathing in the Arno owing to the heat, and . . . represented them hurrying out of the water to dress, and seizing their arms to go to assist their comrades. . . . Among other figures is an old man wearing a crown of ivy to shade his head, trying to pull his stockings on to his wet feet, and hearing the cries of the soldiers and the beating of the drums, he is struggling violently, all his muscles to the tips of his toes, and his contorted mouth showing the effects of his exertion.[38]

The cartoon was eventually torn into fragments by excessive handling and overuse, but the drawing served to enhance the reputation and widespread fame of Michelangelo.

Head to Head with the Pope: The Sistine Chapel

After Pope Alexander VI died, Pope Pius III was in office less than a month when he also passed away. Pius was succeeded by Cardinal Giuliano della Rovere who took the name Julius II. The new pope's main objective was to unite the Papal States and protect them from France and Spain, which wanted to take over parts of Italy. The Italian Wars were a series of military campaigns that occurred during Michelangelo's lifetime between the Papal States, the rival city-states, and the European powers.

These wars were very expensive and often took money away from the new pope's other focus—the transformation of Rome into the beautiful and glorious city it once was. Julius employed the architect Donato Bramante, the painter Raphael, the Florentine builder Giuliano da Sangallo, and then Michelangelo, who was summoned to Rome in 1505.

A significant portion of Michelangelo's life involved his conflict-filled relationship with Julius. These two men were both stubborn and willful characters who often butted heads about art projects but worked together for more than eight years in a type of love/hate association.

The Tomb of Julius

Michelangelo's first commission from Julius was for his tomb, which was to eventually be placed within St. Peter's Basilica. Michelangelo's plans were for a massive monument of marble, standing detached from the walls, rising into three levels, and tapering into a pyramid at the top. Author Lutz Heusinger describes Michelangelo's original plans for the tomb for which he was to be paid ten thousand ducats over the course of five years. According to Heusinger,

> Forty life-size statues were to surround the tomb, which was to be 23 feet (7.01 m) wide, 36 feet, 3 inches (11.05 m) deep, 26 feet, 4 inches (8.03 m) high; . . . the 'Victories' and the 'Slaves' intended for the lower level: . . . Moses and St. Paul, among others, were to have been placed in the middle level, surrounded by representations of examples of the active and contemplative lives. . . . At the summit . . . there was to have been a portrayal of two angels leading the Pope out of his tomb on the day of the Last Judgment.[39]

Michelangelo set out for Carrara to choose the marble blocks for the immense monument and spent eight months there. While he was away, the rebuilding of St. Peter's began with Bramante as the chief architect. This renovation required a huge amount of money, and the pope decided to hold off on the tomb project for a while.

When the ninety-plus wagonloads of marble were cut, transported, and unloaded, Michelangelo ran out of the money advanced to him by the pope. Ascanio Condivi writes that Julius had told Michelangelo to come directly to him if he needed additional funds, so he went to see the pope directly. His Holiness was busy with other matters, so Michelangelo ended up paying the workers for the transportation of the marble out of his own pocket. He expected to be reimbursed by the pope at a later time. Antonio Forcellino notes that Michelangelo spent a large portion of his advance on property investments, and that is why he ran out of money. Again and again Michelangelo returned to see the pope, but each time, Julius would not grant him an audience.

Michelangelo's tomb of Pope Julius II. A dispute between Michelangelo and the pope over payment led to Michelangelo's return to Florence.

Michelangelo got angry, since no one had ever treated him this way. Condivi writes that the young sculptor left Julius a message. He said, "You may tell the Pope that, henceforward, if he wants me, he must look for me elsewhere."[40] Michelangelo then returned home, told his servants to sell his possessions, and rode off to Florence on horseback.

Anger and Forgiveness

Several messengers followed in an attempt to bring Michelangelo forcibly back to Rome, but since he was in Florentine

DUCATS, FLORINS, AND SCUDI

Ducats were twenty-karat gold coins first used in Venice and then throughout Italy. The average salary of a craftsman was no more than 100–120 ducats per year. Rent on a large workshop cost 10 ducats a year. The florin was equivalent to the ducat and used mainly in Florence. The scudo (plural: scudi) was also used in Florence but had slightly less gold content than the florin or ducat.

territory, they could not do so. Instead they asked him to reply to Julius's letter that ordered the sculptor back immediately. Michelangelo responded that since Julius apparently refused to continue with the tomb project, he was free to pursue other assignments. For three months, angry letters were exchanged between the pope and Michelangelo, but nothing was resolved.

In the meantime, the papal forces had conquered Bologna, and the pope visited the city. Michelangelo feared for his own safety. The Florentine cardinal Soderini encouraged the artist to go see Julius and patch up the feud, or his forces could be attacking Florence next. Michelangelo agreed to see the pope in Bologna, provided he was given safe passage, and when they finally met in person, he got down on his knees and begged for forgiveness.

Julius pardoned Michelangelo and also assigned him a new commission in Bologna. He wanted a bronze statue of himself, three times larger than life, to watch over (some said threaten) the city. Michelangelo received one thousand ducats for the statue, which was completed in 1508. (Unfortunately, it was destroyed by an angry mob in 1511). Michelangelo returned to Rome, ready to continue work on Julius's tomb, but the pope had another project in mind.

For the Glory of God and Rome

Both Condivi and Giorgio Vasari write that the architect Bramante had told Julius that it was a bad omen to work on his tomb while he was still alive. He convinced the pope to have Michelangelo paint the giant more than 12,000-square-foot ceiling (1,115 sq. m) of the Sistine Chapel (the pope's chapel and the place where papal elections are held) at the Vatican. Bramante knew full well that the artist was a sculptor and had little experience in fresco painting and coloring. In fact, the last time Michelangelo had painted frescoes was in Domenico Ghirlandaio's workshop as a young man. *Fresco* was the term used to describe a type of painting directly on the wet plaster of a wall or ceiling where the colors penetrated and were absorbed before the plaster hardened. According to Condivi and Vasari, Michelangelo was Bramante's main rival in Rome for

A re-creation of Michelangelo's scaffolding was used in the 1965 film *The Agony and the Ecstasy* starring Charlton Heston (pictured) as the artist. Michelangelo used footbridges and stepped arches across the ceiling's void to give painters and plasterers decks to work on and access to every part of the Sistine Chapel's ceiling.

art commissions from the pope. Bramante wanted Michelangelo to fail, and even if he succeeded, he expected the pope and Michelangelo to have numerous disagreements.

Michelangelo used every means possible to excuse himself from the Sistine Chapel commission. He recommended the well-known painter Raphael for the work. He insisted he was a sculptor, not a painter. The more Michelangelo tried to get out of the assignment, the more the pope insisted he do it. Finally, Michelangelo agreed.

His first task was to build scaffolding that could support buckets of water, bags of sand and lime, and the weight of the painters sixty feet above the ground. The chapel was still to be used as a place of worship by the pope and senior officials, so the scaffolding could not block the aisles. According to Ross King, Michelangelo designed "a series of footbridges that spanned the chapel from the level of the windows" using "a number of stepped arches . . . that served as linked bridges across the void, giving the painters and plasterers decks on which to work as well as access to every part of the ceiling."[41]

Spaces on the Ceiling

The original design of the Sistine ceiling fresco was to be of the twelve Apostles, but when Michelangelo voiced his objection to Julius, the pope gave him complete freedom to choose his subjects. Michelangelo divided the curved barrel vault of the ceiling into nine basic scenes from the Old Testament, including the division of light from darkness, the creation of the sun, moon, and planets, the separation of land from the oceans, the creation of Adam and Eve, and the Great Flood. He focused on the human figure with minimal landscape, including what King describes as the world-famous "finger-to-finger transmission of the spark of life from God to Adam."[42]

The ceiling also has four large triangular-shaped pendentives in each corner between the arches, rounded half-moon or crescent-shaped spaces above the windows called lunettes, small triangular-shaped spaces above the windows called spandrels, as well as rectangular panels. Prophets from the Old Testament and sibyls, prophetic women who foretold the future, were

The restored Sistine Chapel's ceiling. The ceiling's surface was curved, and Michelangelo used a painting technique called foreshortening in which parts of figures nearest the viewer are painted larger than those farther away to create the illusion of three-dimensional space and distance.

painted in the rectangular panels. The lunettes were filled with paintings of ninety-one ancestors of Jesus, including twenty-five women. This depiction of Jesus's female ancestors (other than Mary) was a first in Christian religious art. The large pendentives show scenes of great Jewish figures of the bible—Moses, Esther, David, and Judith. The triangular shaped spandrels were all filled with domestic scenes of family life.

Much of the surface of the ceiling was curved, and a painting technique called foreshortening was often utilized. Since the ceiling would be viewed at a distance from the ground or at angles, those parts of figures nearest to the viewers were usually painted larger than those further away to create the illusion of three-dimensional fullness and distance. Throughout the painting Michelangelo included adult nude figures (ignudi) and naked little cupids and angels (putti) that appear to hold up, sit upon, or pose near various ceiling ornamentation such as medallions, cornices, and moldings. There are also a number of what King describes as "a series of grotesque nudes . . . smaller in size than the ignudi . . . [that] . . . kick, squirm, and scream in confined areas."[43]

Preparation and Hard Work

Michelangelo made more than one thousand drawings of his vision of the Sistine Chapel ceiling before he ever started to paint. Contrary to popular belief, he did not paint the chapel ceiling while lying flat on his back on the scaffolding. In fact, he and his assistants (who worked on backgrounds and minor figures) stood upright and bent their necks at various angles to paint. Since Michelangelo completed the major figures on the ceiling, his neck and shoulder muscles were often strained and aching, and his eyesight was affected for a time. "This posture," writes George Bull, "left him for a while unable to read a letter without holding it above his head."[44]

The work on the ceiling took a physical and emotional toll on Michelangelo, who wrote a sonnet about his unhappy experiences to his friend Giovanni di Benedetto from Pistoia in 1510.

> I've grown a goitre by dwelling in this den—
> As cats from stagnant streams in Lombardy,
> Or in what other land they hap to be—
> Which drives the belly close beneath the chin:
> My beard turns up to heaven; my nape falls in,
> Fixed on my spine: my breast-bone visibly
> Grows like a harp: a rich embroidery
> Bedews my face from brush-drops thick and thin. . . .
> Come then, Giovanni, try
> To succour my dead pictures and my fame,
> Since foul I fare and painting is my shame.[45]

"**I** see myself so ugly," writes Michelangelo in one of his poems. The great artist knew he was a homely man and portrayed himself that way in his own artwork. In one of the pendentives on the Sistine Chapel ceiling, the Jewish heroine Judith cuts off the head of Holofernes, the commander of the enemy troops. Judith carried away "a bearded, scowling, flat-nosed, disembodied head that served as Michelangelo's less-than-heroic image of himself," writes art historian Ross King and author of *Michelangelo & the Pope's Ceiling.*

The prophet Jeremiah was painted by Michelangelo as a slumping figure on his throne with a long grey beard, staring at the ground with his head resting on his chin. This is considered to be another of Michelangelo's self-portraits. But Jeremiah does not have an ugly face. The prophet's face is sad and pessimistic, much the way Michelangelo felt during the last, difficult period of painting the Sistine Chapel fresco with his financial and family difficulties.

King writes that the famous Renaissance painter Raphael, after seeing Michelangelo's Sistine Chapel ceiling, added another figure to his painting *The School of Athens,* both as an homage to the moody genius as well as a dig. The face of the philosopher Heraclitus, known for his doctrine of universal change as well as what King describes as "bitter scorn for all rivals" is very similar to that of Michelangelo, who King notes was "surly . . . [and] remote." In

the painting Heraclitus is "a self-absorbed, downcast figure with black hair and a beard," writes King, "[who] . . . rests his head on his fist as he scribbles distractedly on a piece of paper, utterly oblivious to the philosophical debates raging about him."

Ross King. *Michelangelo & The Pope's Ceiling.* New York: Walker, 2003, pp. 233–235.

The slumping figure of the prophet Jeremiah in one of the Sistine's panels is thought to be yet another self-portrait that hints at a difficult time in Michelangelo's life.

While Michelangelo worked on the chapel ceiling, Julius often left Rome for long periods of time to conduct various military campaigns in Bologna or Venice in an attempt to rid Italy of Europeans. Whenever Julius returned, he visited Michelangelo to see how the work on the ceiling was progressing and questioned him regularly as to when it would be finished. Michelangelo would then reply, "When I can."[46]

Both Condivi and Vasari relate an incident that occurred when Michelangelo asked the pope if he could go home to Florence to spend the feast of St. John with his family and requested money for his journey. Again, the pope asked, "When will this chapel be ready?" and Michelangelo again replied, "When I can get it done, Holy Father." Vasari writes,

> The Pope struck him with his mace [staff], repeating, "When I can, when I can, I will make you finish it!" Michelangelo, however, returned to his house to prepare for his journey to Florence, when the Pope sent Cursio, his chamberlain, with five hundred scudi to appease him and excuse the Pope. . . . As Michelangelo knew the Pope, and was really devoted to him, he laughed, especially as such things always turned to his advantage, and the Pope did everything to retain his goodwill.[47]

Word of a Masterpiece Spreads

When Michelangelo completed half of the ceiling, he took the scaffolding down and, at the request of the pope, opened up the chapel to the public. People came out in large numbers to view the half-finished masterpiece. Then Michelangelo put the scaffolding back up in the second half of the chapel and completed the remaining parts of the ceiling in twenty months, often working nights by candlelight and without cartoons in the smaller spaces.

Once he mastered the fresco techniques on the first few panels, he was able to work more efficiently and with confidence on the rest of the ceiling. The figures painted on the second half of the ceiling were larger and seemed more con-

fined in the spaces. More than 340 figures were painted on the ceiling in unusually bright yellows, greens, oranges, blues, reds, and whites.

All of Italy was following the work of Michelangelo in Rome. Wealthy art lovers and collectors would often go up the scaffolding to see the ceiling and chat. Many visitors were so impressed by Michelangelo's talent they discussed future commissions with him.

In July 1512 Michelangelo wrote to his brother Buonaroto, "I toil harder than any man who ever was, unwell and with enormous effort; and yet I have the patience to reach the desired end."[48] Another letter written to Ludovico in October 1512 was full of self-pity. Michelangelo complained, "I lead a

The altar in the Sistine Chapel. Michelangelo completed his masterpiece on October 31, 1512, four years and four weeks after he began it. People came from all over to view the amazing work, and Michelangelo became a living legend.

When Michelangelo had to pay the workmen for transporting the Carrara marble to Rome for Julius's tomb out of his own pocket, he was also pressured for money by his father, Ludovico, and two of his brothers, Buonarroto and Giovansimone. His brothers wanted Michelangelo to financially back them in a business, or find them jobs in Rome. According to art historian John T. Spike in his book *Young Michelangelo: The Path to the Sistine,* "Michelangelo pushed back firmly, pleading poverty as he always did: 'A few days ago I wrote Ludovico and told him that I have four hundred large ducats worth of marble here and that I owe a hundred and forty ducats on it, so that I haven't got a quattrino [penny]. I'm telling you the same thing, so that you may see that for the time being, I cannot help you.'"

Spike explains that Ludovico knew that Michelangelo's bank accounts in Florence and Rome were "brimming over with . . . ducats." He knew that his son often lied to him about money as he did to his son. Despite his wealth, it never seemed enough since, according to Spike, Michelangelo felt constant stress about money. Spike writes, "He began to ask Julius repeatedly, insistently, obsessively, for more money," and this resulted in their first major falling out in 1506. In the meantime, he continued to purchase property near Florence with Ludovico acting as his representative.

John T. Spike. *Young Michelangelo: The Path to the Sistine.* New York: Vendome, 2010, p. 198.

miserable existence. I live wearied by stupendous labours and beset by a thousand anxieties. And thus have I lived for some fifteen years now and never an hour's happiness have I had. And all this I have done in order to help you, though you have never either recognized or believed it."[49]

The Sistine Chapel ceiling was finally completed on October 31, 1512, four years and four weeks after Michelangelo first began. Early nineteenth-century German author Johann Wolfgang von Goethe wrote, "Until you have seen the Sistine Chapel, you can have no adequate conception of what man is capable of accomplishing."[50] Forcellino declares, "What Michelangelo had achieved with the statue of *David* not ten years earlier was now repeated, with the painting of the chapel ceiling creating an even greater sensation. At the age of thirty-seven, the ambitious Florentine had become a living legend."[51]

Medicis In, Julius Out

While Michelangelo was finishing up the ceiling, the Medicis regained control of the Florentine government. Four months after the unveiling of the ceiling, Pope Julius II died in February 1513. Before his death, Julius made it clear to his heirs and family that he wished Michelangelo to continue work on his tomb and issued a papal bull [public order] that allocated ten thousand ducats for the tomb.

Michelangelo and the executors of Julius's estate soon signed a contract that increased his total payment to 16,500 ducats (minus what he had already received). They agreed that the tomb would be completed in seven years but be attached to a wall of St. Peter's instead of freestanding. Michelangelo was eager to return to what he believed was his primary talent—working as a sculptor.

The Tragedy of the Tomb

The large amount of white marble that had been set aside years before was transported to Michelangelo's workshop, and he began to carve several statues for the tomb—the *Moses* (7 feet 8½ inches (2.34m) high), the *Dying Slave* (7 feet 6⅛ inches (2.29m) high), and the *Rebellious Slave* (7 feet ⅝ inch (2.15m) high). However, he was again taken away from the project by the newly elected pope, Cardinal Giovanni de' Medici, who took the name of Leo X in March 1513. This was the same Giovanni who was a childhood friend of Michelangelo. Despite the fact that the famous artist had supported the republic in Florence and opposed Medici rule, Leo turned out to be an accommodating patron of the arts and supporter of Michelangelo.

Michelangelo's *Rebellious Slave* was not placed in the tomb of Julius as originally intended and now rests in the Louvre in Paris.

Over the next thirty-two years, the renowned artist attempted to work on the tomb of Julius, but was often called away by various popes to work on other commissions. Five additional contracts were modified and signed by Julius's heirs, and each time the size of the tomb was reduced. Then the Rovere heirs decided to sue Michelangelo for the money they had already paid him. A negotiated settlement was reached, and still another contract was signed. The tomb was decreased even further in size, and it was agreed that it should be placed in the Church of San Pietro in Vincoli, where Juilius II had served as cardinal, instead of in St. Peter's.

Several popes intervened to excuse Michelangelo from working on the tomb until the Rovere family finally agreed in a 1542 contract to allow other sculptors to finish the statues with Michelangelo's *Moses* as the centerpiece. The *Dying Slave* and *Rebellious Slave* were not placed on the tomb. After passing through private hands, the two statues are now on exhibit in the Louvre in Paris. Joachim Poeschke writes, "The *Dying Slave* . . . depicts exhaustion and mute surrender." Referring to the *Rebellious Slave*, Poeschke declares, "The pose is not one of sinuous extension, but rather contraction. Strength is not seen to be ebbing away but rather to be concentrated to the utmost against the restraining bonds."[52] In 1542 an older, more spiritual Michelangelo sculpted figures of biblical heroines Rachel and Leah. Art historians believe the two represented faith and good works, or as Vasari and Condivi note, the active life and the contemplative life. These two figures replaced the slave figures on the tomb of Julius, and historians differ as to whether Michelangelo or another sculptor completed the figures.

The central statue of Moses is described by Umberto Baldini as having "enormous strength . . . [a] robust fluctuating play of lights and shadows."[53] Condivi notes the face of Moses is both tender and terrifying, while Vasari refers to it as being holy and formidable. Moses holds the tablets of the law under one arm and his flowing beard in the fingers of his other hand. Since Michelangelo had completed only a small portion of the tomb, he was paid three thousand ducats. The completed structure was finally unveiled at the Church of San Pietro in 1545, nearly forty years after its inception.

The tragedy of the tomb was in the length of time it took to complete, the huge reduction in size from Michelangelo's original concept in 1506, and the fact that the great artist only had a minimal role in its final form. Whereas Michelangelo was saddened by the events surrounding the tomb, he was kept busy by a series of family art commissions from Pope Leo X and the Medicis, who remained in power for many years.

Florence and the Medicis: In and Out of Power

The Medici family had become extremely powerful in Italy. Leo X was now the pope as well as the leader of Florence. His brother Giuliano was made head of the papal forces. His cousin Giulio was the archbishop of Florence and then a cardinal, and his nephew Lorenzo controlled the day-to-day matters in Florence in the pope's absence. Despite Michelangelo's support for the Florentine republic, the Medicis looked favorably upon him, perhaps remembering their shared childhood and the patronage and warm friendship of Lorenzo the Magnificent toward the young artist.

The Fiasco of the Facade

Leo X was the first Florentine pope, and he focused his artistic aspirations on his home city and powerful family rather than the Vatican in Rome. He commissioned Michelangelo, a fellow Florentine, to design and complete the facade (front wall) of the Church of San Lorenzo in Florence in 1516. Michelangelo agreed to complete the project in eight years and was to be paid forty thousand ducats. George Bull writes, "The work . . . included eight fluted marble columns rising to the first cornice and framing the three doors of the church and a total of twenty-two statues, of which the six on the storey over the door were to be over life-size seated figures in bronze . . . and seven marble scenes in low relief, five square panels and two round."[54]

Michelangelo traveled to Carrara to pick out the marble for the new project and while there received a letter from the pope telling him to get the marble in the Pietrasanta Mountains near the town of Seravezza instead. Despite the fact that Michelangelo believed it was too difficult and expensive to get to this new marble site, Leo insisted. A road had to be built several miles through the mountains to get there. Bad weather, inexperienced marble cutters and quarrymen, and accidents with the marble blocks caused numerous delays. According to Giorgio Vasari, Michelangelo "spent many years in quarrying marble . . . [and] . . . it dragged on so long that the money appointed for it by the Pope was consumed by the war."[55] Finally, in 1520 Leo canceled the project.

Michelangelo was shocked and upset at losing the commission and wrote a letter, according to Bull, to a lawyer or legal clerk in Florence to set the record straight and account for the eighteen hundred ducats he had already spent on the facade. In the letter he says,

> I have . . . not charg[ed] to Pope Leo . . . for the wooden model for the said façade, which I sent to Rome; nor am I putting to his account the period of three years that I have lost over this; nor am I putting to his account that I have been ruined over the said work of San Lorenzo; nor am I putting to his account the gross insult of having brought me here to do the said work, and then taking it from me; . . . nor do I charge to his account my house in Rome that I have left, including marble, furniture and completed work, which has deteriorated to the amount of over 500 ducats.[56]

With the Vatican short of cash and fighting a war in Lombardy (northern Italy and Milan) against the French, Leo sold indulgences to raise money for his various projects. Indulgences were partial reductions of punishment for sin in

This painting by Jacopa da Empoli depicts Michelangelo presenting his plan for the facade of the Church of San Lorenzo to Pope Leo X. Due to war expenses the pope canceled the commission in 1520.

return for charitable contributions to the church. In addition, lower offices were given out to those who had made generous donations. This "financial opportunism,"[57] as Bull describes it, was the basis for Martin Luther's criticism of the church, the subsequent Reformation, and the formation of Protestantism.

In Praise of Family and Florence

Leo's brother Guiliano (the Duke of Nemours) died in 1516, and his nephew Lorenzo (the Duke of Urbino) died in 1519. Leo was forty-five years old (as was Michelangelo) in 1520. He became more aware of his own mortality as he approached the later years of his life, so he decided on a new art project to glorify his family. The church facade was out, and a new sacristy, Medici tomb, and library were now high priorities at San Lorenzo. The library would contain the late Lorenzo the Magnificent's collection of rare books, statues, and letters. The tomb would hold the remains of Lorenzo, who had died in 1492; Lorenzo's brother Guiliano, who was murdered in 1478; Leo's brother Guiliano; and his nephew Lorenzo. The commission was offered to Michelangelo, possibly to make up for his disappointment with the facade.

While Michelangelo was involved in the design of the Medici tomb, Leo died suddenly on December 1, 1521, at the age of forty-six. The new pope, Adrian VI of the Netherlands (also known as Hadrian), was not at all interested in art or Michelangelo. Adrian was careful with finances and tried to limit Medici power. Michelangelo stopped work on the San Lorenzo projects and resumed work on the tomb of Julius. Adrian's term as pope ended with his premature death in September 1523 after only eighteen months as pope. He was succeeded by Cardinal Giulio de' Medici, who took the name Clement VII, the second Florentine to be elected pope. William E. Wallace declares, "Adrian's passing . . . was accompanied by a collective sigh of relief, especially from the artists who had enjoyed Leo X's liberality."[58]

Another Medici Pope

The new pope was as eager to support the arts as had been his cousin Leo X. After consulting with Michelangelo, Clement took him away from work on the tomb of Julius and put him back to work on the Medici projects, both as a builder and a sculptor. At the work site in 1525, the fifty-year-old Michelangelo worked simultaneously on the chapel and library and supervised a workforce of over one hundred stonecutters and carvers.

Michelangelo introduced various aspects of Mannerism, the style of art that broke away from the classical forms of balance and symmetry, and emphasized exaggerated twists and distortions of the human body. He used Mannerist characteristics not only in his sculpture but in the architecture itself, varying perspective, and using columns built into the walls that often extended over several stories. Michelangelo sculpted more than six statues at a time, going from one to the other. Frequently, after a fourteen-hour workday the artist worked into the night by candlelight. His only day of rest was Sunday, when he visited his father and brothers in Florence.

Wallace quotes Blais de Vignere, a Frenchman who described watching Michelangelo later in life at work on a statue:

> I have seen Michelangelo, although more than sixty years old and no longer among the most robust, knock off more chips of a very hard marble in a quarter of an hour than three young stone carvers could have done in three or four, an almost incredible thing to one who has not seen it; and I thought the whole work would fall to pieces because he moved with such impetuosity and fury, knocking to the floor large chunks three and four fingers thick with a single blow so precisely aimed that if he had gone even minimally further than necessary, he risked losing it all.[59]

The Medici Chapel and the Laurentian Library

Referring to the Medici Chapel, Wallace declares that "Michelangelo fashioned a lavish environment in which marble tombs project from the walls and figures adorning those tombs appear to slip from their supports." Michelangelo's original concept called for four tombs, many statues, and much ornamentation. The tomb he finally completed after several years was in an "unfinished state," but is still considered one of his masterpieces. According to Wallace, "The two Medici dukes . . . [Lorenzo and Guiliano] . . . are seated in shallow niches above the sarcophagi that contain their remains. . . . Four nude allegorical

THE REFORMATION, MARTIN LUTHER, AND THE PRINTING PRESS

There had always been objections to church doctrine and practices. During the Renaissance, criticism greatly increased, especially against the abuses of the church, the emphasis on money, and the general harshness of church policies. The center of reform was the University of Wittenberg in Germany. It was here that Martin Luther (1483–1546), a professor of theology at the university, protested against church indulgences by posting his Ninety-Five Theses on the castle church wall. Luther attacked the papacy, stating the pope had no power over secular leaders, and declared that the Holy Father did not have the final interpretation of scripture. Luther rejected the sacraments except as aids to faith and wrote that priests did not have the sole authority to intervene between God and the individual. He believed that salvation came through faith alone, totally rejected papal authority, and was formally excommunicated from the church in 1521.

The invention of the printing press helped to spread the opinions of Martin Luther throughout Europe, and his positions became increasingly popular among all classes of people. His principles became the basis for Lutheranism, a branch of Protestantism that arose when it became evident that reforms could not be carried out within the Roman Catholic Church.

Pope Leo X's corruption and moral disregard led to the Protestant Reformation. Martin Luther started it when he posted his Ninety-Five Theses on religion on a church wall, rejecting papal authority. Luther was excommunicated from the church in 1521.

Michelangelo's design for the Laurentian Library included a triple staircase (above) in the lobby that led to the reading room (opposite page) with a wide aisle and reading desks. It is considered one of the artist's greatest architectural works.

figures recline on the curved sarcophagi lids. Traditionally these represent Day and Night, Dawn and Dusk—a sort of figural meditation on time."[60] The Medici Chapel artwork by Michelangelo dealt with the theme of the consistent and unstoppable passage of time and the shortness of human life in relation to it.

The Laurentian Library was built in the same San Lorenzo Church complex as the chapel to house the books and manuscripts of the Medicis. The lobby of the library is one of the most beautiful and impressive of Michelangelo's architectural works, dominated by a triple staircase, which fills more than half of the chamber. "This is an entire room," writes Wallace, "devoted to the transitional experience of moving from the noisy exterior to the quiet serenity of the library."[61] The staircases lead

into the reading room by means of a central, wide aisle, flanked on both sides by beautiful wooden reading desks and carved wooden ceiling panels. There are two desks to each large stone-framed window, which allows abundant light to study the rare items kept at the library. "To sit at one of the carved walnut desks," declares Wallace, "is to become a part of the building."[62]

Rome Under Siege

Francis I of France and the Holy Roman emperor and king of Spain, Charles V, had been fighting for control of Italy since 1521. The French were defeated in 1525, and Francis signed the Treaty of Madrid in 1526. But Francis repudiated this treaty and joined with Pope Clement; Henry VIII of England;

and the Dukes of Venice, Milan, and Florence in the League of Cognac to oppose the Holy Roman emperor. The French and papal forces, however, were no match for the imperial troops of Charles.

The emperor's soldiers had not been paid and wanted the spoils of war. They persuaded their commanders to march southward toward Rome, destroying and looting all towns in their way. The imperial army was made up of Spanish and German soldiers, most of whom were angry Lutherans who wanted revenge against the papacy in Rome and to steal the riches of the Eternal City. The troops entered Rome on May 6, 1527, and held siege there for more than a week. It was a brutal bloodbath, and Clement was taken prisoner.

When the citizens of Florence heard news of what had happened in Rome, they rose up on May 16, forced the Medicis out of the city, and reestablished the Florentine Republic. After seven months of captivity, Clement was restored to power and agreed to advance the peace, reform the church, and deal with the new Lutheran faith of the Reformation. In the treaty signed by Clement and Charles, the pope agreed to officially crown the Holy Roman emperor in a public ceremony and give him control of Naples. Charles wanted this public ceremony to demonstrate the pope's deference to him, thus convincing the pope's large number of followers to accept Charles's authority. In return, Charles agreed to restore the Medicis' rule in Florence. The French signed a separate peace agreement.

Clement openly crowned Charles the Holy Roman emperor in February 1530 in Bologna, and the pope then turned to his home city of Florence to exact revenge on those who had ousted the Medicis. One of those who had supported the republic was Michelangelo, who had cut back his work on the Medici commissions during that uncertain time period between 1527 and 1530. Wallace writes, "Despite Clement's effort to dissuade him, Michelangelo elected to side with his native city, because, above all, he was a Florentine with deeply republican loyalties. In Florence's hour of need, he was appointed director of the city's fortifications, and thus he now devoted himself to resisting the very man who had been his pope, patron, and strongest supporter during the previous ten years."[63]

THE SACKING OF ROME

On May 6, 1527, the troops of Holy Roman emperor Charles V occupied the center of Christianity for the express purpose of looting, killing, and destroying the people and riches of Rome and the Vatican. Author and journalist George Bull in his book *Michelangelo: A Biography* describes the terrible scene:

> Positions were taken up on the Piazza Navona by the Spaniards and on the Campo dei Fiori by the Germans. But, soon after, the troops broke away and massive looting started. The sacrilegious Germans and savage Spaniards, it was told in Florence, had run wild in search of booty from the rich stores of cardinals, courtiers and merchants, respecting nobody and nothing, however sacred. Prelates (clerics) had been mounted on asses and mules in their vestments and tormented, tortured to death or held for ransom, mocked, and reviled. Women, including nuns, had been seized and raped. Churches had been vandalized and despoiled. Whole libraries had perished, and papal manuscripts had been used as litter for horses. After the ravening hordes of soldiers had done their worst, the peasants had come in for the pickings among the corpses, the fires and the ruins.
>
> Pope Clement could have destroyed the bridges leading into the city and put up a defense but he neglected to do so. Clement was captured and imprisoned for seven months. He then made peace with Charles and was restored to power.

George Bull. *Michelangelo: A Biography.* New York: St. Martin's, 1995, p. 205.

Target: Florence

The Florentine Republic made an effort to militarily prepare themselves against the troops of the Holy Roman emperor and the papal forces of Clement. Michelangelo was named governor-general of fortifications for the city, and he sat on

Florence's governing council, yet he never entirely stopped working on the San Lorenzo projects. Bull writes that "around the hill of San Miniato, rising high over Florence and commanding a broad sweep of countryside to the south-east beyond the Arno, he was throwing a circle of huge earthworks to support the artillery needed to halt the enemy and bombard its siegeworks."[64] Michelangelo used the tall bell tower of the church as a lookout point and built elevated artillery platforms. He used cannons, defensive walls, and angular structures in the city's defenses. He also ordered bales of wool and heavy mattresses suspended by ropes to protect the bell tower from enemy cannon fire.

After he had completed the tasks of fortifying the city to the best of his ability, Michelangelo secretly fled to Venice. He feared for his life from those who did not like his previous close relationship with the Medicis. Then he had a change of heart and returned to his native city, where he remained during the siege. The republic was cut off from food and supplies for many months, and there were many deaths from disease and hunger. After seven months, an agreement was reached between Florentine emissaries, Clement, and Charles V. The Medicis took

The siege of Florence in 1530. Michelangelo was governor-general of the fortifications of the city. After the siege Alessandro de' Medici wanted to execute him, but Pope Clement VII intervened, pardoning Michelangelo in late 1530.

control of the city and set out to punish those who had opposed their family rule.

Michelangelo was in a difficult situation. Those in favor of the republic distrusted him because he had fled the city (even though he did return) and had never cut his Medici connections entirely. The Medicis were unhappy because he had supported the republic and worked on the city's fortifications against them. The fifty-five-year-old Michelangelo went into hiding before the city surrendered. He was particularly hated by the new Florence governor, Alessandro de' Medici, who regarded the great artist as a traitor, and orders were given for his execution. Clement, however, did not want any harm to come to Michelangelo. By the end of 1530, the artist was pardoned, set free, and returned to his work at San Lorenzo, with the pope intervening on his behalf to hold the Rovere heirs at bay in the Julius II tomb contract.

Personal Setbacks

The plague had struck Florence in the summer of 1528, and Michelangelo lost his beloved brother Buonarroto in July of that year. Buonarroto was survived by his wife, Bartolommea; two sons, Lionardo and Simone; and a daughter, Francesca. Michelangelo paid for the funeral and, as was customary, returned Bartolommea's dowry. Six-year-old Lionardo, who stayed with Michelangelo for seven months, and two-year-old Simone, who later died, went to live with Ludovico, who was now in his eighties, and nine-year-old Francesca was cared for by nuns in a local convent. (The father's family ordinarily took custody of the children in Renaissance Italy).

Michelangelo feared Alessandro, who was rumored to be Clement's illegitimate son. When Alessandro was made the first hereditary (duke of Florence for life) by Charles in 1531, Michelangelo's ties to the city began to unravel. Alessandro wanted to consult with Michelangelo on the best site for a fortress to defend the city. Michelangelo, however, suspected this was a ruse and that Alessandro planned to kill him. Michelangelo refused to go unless ordered by Clement. This angered Alessandro even more.

Then Ludovico Buonarroti died in 1531 at the age of eighty-seven, and Michelangelo's ties to Florence were never

*A*round 1519–1520, Michelangelo took on a contract to sculpt a risen Christ for the Church of Santa Maria sopra Minerva. The original marble block was found to have black veins and had to be abandoned. The life-size standing nude carried a cross and was 80 3/4 inches high (2.05m). *Risen Christ* (also known as *Christ Carrying the Cross*) was mostly sculpted by Michelangelo, but it was shipped to Rome and finished by an assistant, Pietro Urbano. Urbano did an inferior job of finishing the face, hands, and feet, and another sculptor, Federigo Frizzi, corrected the damage. Professor of art his-

tory Joachim Poeschke in his book *Michelangelo and His World: Sculpture of the Italian Renaissance* writes, "It was certainly unusual to depict the risen Christ completely naked and unheard-of to provide him with a robust and classically beautiful body with no traces of wounds." Years later, the sculpture was provided with a loincloth and wounds.

Joachim Poeschke. *Michelangelo and His World: Sculpture of the Italian Renaissance.* New York: Harry N. Abrams, 1992, p. 100.

Michelangelo's Risen Christ was found to have defects in the marble so he abandoned it when it was nearly finished. Other sculptors finished the face, hands, and feet. Years later the wounds and the loincloth were added so as to not offend religious sensibilities.

the same. He grieved strongly for his lost family members. That same year, he became very ill from too much hard work without proper rest or diet. The pope ordered him to cut back on all work except the Medici projects until his health improved. A poem written by Michelangelo about the deaths of his brother and father reveals his deep grief:

Deep grief such woe unto my heart did give,
I thought it wept the bitter pain away,
And tears and moans would let my spirit live.

But fate renews the fount of grief to-day,
And feeds each hidden root and secret vein
By death that doth still harder burden lay.
I of thy parting speak; and yet again
For him, of thee who later left me here,
My tongue and pen shall speak the separate pain.
He was my brother, thou our father dear;
Love clung to him and duty bound to thee,
Nor can I tell which loss I hold most near.[65]

In 1532, in a trip to Rome to sign still another Rovere contract concerning the tomb of Julius, the fifty-seven-year-old artist (an old man by the standard of the times) met the very handsome twenty-three-year-old Tommaso de' Cavalieri, who became a close friend through the remainder of Michelangelo's life. He also met twice with Clement to discuss the cartoon for a new project, a fresco for the huge altar wall of the Sistine Chapel. The pope wanted a painting of the day of the Last Judgment, the day of Christ's Second Coming according to Christian tradition. When Clement died in September 1534, Michelangelo lost his last great ally among the Medicis and decided it was time to leave Florence permanently. In 1534 he headed to Rome where the new pope, Paul III, wanted to continue with Clement's project. In Rome, his newfound friend Cavalieri also awaited him. With Clement's death, Michelangelo, according to Joachim Poeschke, "was released from further obligations to the Medici. He immediately stopped work on the Medici Chapel and the San Lorenzo library and moved to Rome for good."[66]

5 Nel Frattempo di Nuovo a Roma ... Meanwhile, Back in Rome ... the Last Judgment

Michelangelo bid arrivederci (good-bye) to Florence and returned to the Eternal City in 1534 at the age of fifty-nine. The new pope, Paul III, was anxious for him to begin work on the *Last Judgment*, the fresco for the altar wall of the Sistine Chapel, originally conceived by Clement. This large space was 66 feet by 33 feet (20.12m x 10.06m). The completed painting took six years to finish and included more than 350 figures awaiting the judgment of Christ.

William E. Wallace declares, "Paul's long pontificate [term as pope], from 1534 to 1549, was a glorious period for Michelangelo. He was at the apex of his fame, surrounded by friends and admirers, and working for one of the most discerning patrons of all time. . . . Michelangelo turned increasingly to architecture and helped transform a dilapidated ancient city into a modern Christian capital."[67]

A Different World

Paul officially appointed Michelangelo as "supreme architect, painter, and sculptor of the Apostolic Palace"[68] (the official residence of the pope at the Vatican), and he received a regular income from the position. He immersed himself in the fresco of the *Last Judgment* all the while working in the shadow of the Sistine Chapel ceiling that he had completed more than twenty years before. By 1535 the world had changed and so had Michelangelo. The chapel ceiling was composed of separate scenes with a particular point of view, but the *Last Judgment* was one huge scene with the single theme of divine punishment, or resurrection and salvation. The Roman Catholic Church was dominant and unchallenged when the ceiling was painted in the early sixteenth century. Now there was the Protestant Reformation and the church's response to Protestantism, the Counter-Reformation.

The Council of Trent became the focal point of the Counter-Reformation and was first convened by Paul in 1545. The council worked to correct abuses of the church and clarify beliefs. The first session under Paul specifically defined and interpreted Scripture, concepts of original sin, the sacraments, baptism, preaching, alms collecting, and the specific duties and responsibilities of the levels of clergy. Other sessions took place in 1551–1552 and 1562–1563. It was the third session in 1563 that expressly forbade nudity in religious works of art.

The Last Judgment

This immense fresco was divided into three main rows of figures. The top row was heaven with the figures of Jesus, the Virgin Mary, and saints, prophets, martyrs, and apostles. The middle row was filled with trumpet-blowing angels who determined whether souls ascended to heaven or descended to hell. In the bottom row, souls were transported to hell or resurrected. The main figure was Christ, who was a bit larger than the other figures in the painting. Antonio Forcellino writes, "[Christ] is . . . in the act of rising to his feet, drawn along by the gesture of his arm, which sets off a whole vortex of surrounding figures. As a result of this motion, the damned are cast downwards and the saved are propelled upwards, while the ranks of the elect, saints and martyrs . . . surround Christ."[69] According to Wallace, "In the lower left of the vast fresco, we see the dead issuing forth from graves . . . the reborn bodies are physically assisted in their ascent to heaven by angels . . . just

Michelangelo's vision of the day of judgment, damnation, and resurrection, *Last Judgment,* adorns a wall of the Sistine Chapel. Viewed for the first time in 1541, it immediately caused controversy because of its depiction of nude holy men and women.

as, on the opposite side of the fresco, the damned are violently thrust into hell."[70]

Michelangelo focused on every possible movement, contortion, and physical characteristic, gesture, and emotion of the nude human body in the *Last Judgment,* including cruelty, greed, evil, fear, virtue, forgiveness, charity, and joy. A papal official, Biagio da Cesena, criticized the painting, and according to Giorgio Vasari, "said it was a disgrace to have put so many nudes in such a place, and that the work was better suited to a bathing-place or an inn than a chapel."[71] That remark made Michelangelo so angry he painted Biagio's likeness onto Minos, judge of souls in hell, with a snake wrapped around his body.

Michelangelo painted his own face on St. Bartholomew, located just below Christ. Bartholomew was flayed alive because he would not renounce his faith. The figure of Bartholomew holds a knife and his own skin. George Bull writes that Michelangelo painted the faces and features of many of those he knew on the figures of the fresco, including Tommaso de' Cavalieri as St. Sebastian holding the arrows that martyred him.

Everyone Is a Critic

Last Judgment was viewed by the public for the first time on December 25, 1541, when Michelangelo was sixty-six years old. The painting was praised and studied by fellow artists and students, and the public was awed and impressed by Michelangelo's vision of the day of judgment, damnation, and resurrection. Soon, copies, prints, reproductions, and woodcuts were circulating everywhere. Like Biagio, however, pious members of the church were shocked by what they considered the inappropriate nudity of holy men and women.

"The perfect beauty of the anatomies and the affecting restraint of the gestures immediately define this painting as the most beautiful and unrepeatable work of art produced in Christendom," declares Forcellino. "But with equal suddenness, it also attracted criticisms of the artist for its obscenity and lack of faith—for the nudes and the representation of saints and angels as human beings." Forcellino writes that Michelangelo believed that "the beauty of Man . . . is a product of the greatness of God, and it is impossible to glorify God without showing it."[72] Paul was not concerned about the condemnations, which continued until the end of Michelangelo's life.

Paintings in the Pauline

The Pauline Chapel was built by Paul (and named after him) at the Vatican not far from the Sistine Chapel (which was named after Pope Sixtus IV). Paul wanted Michelangelo to paint two frescoes on the side walls so his chapel would also be remembered by future generations. Each wall was about 20 feet x 20 feet (6.1m x 6.1m). One fresco was to depict the conversion of Saul and the other the crucifixion of St. Peter.

Michelangelo was now an elderly man and worked intermittently on these two paintings from 1542 to 1550 (until he was seventy-five years of age). The great artist was still sharp and productive, having outlived many of his peers. Despite the fact that the space was much smaller than the *Last Judgment*, Michelangelo took longer to complete the frescoes because of his advanced age. They were the last paintings he ever completed.

The *Conversion of Saul* was one of two frescoes Michelangelo did for the Pauline Chapel in Rome. He finished them at the age of seventy-five, and they would be the last paintings he would complete.

The *Conversion of Saul* (also known as the *Conversion of St. Paul*) is often flooded with direct, natural sunlight, which adds to the effect of the painting. Wallace writes, "Descending as a bolt of lightning from heaven . . . Christ causes Saul . . . to fall from his horse, which is now leaping in terror into the background."[73]

The *Crucifixion of St. Peter*

In contrast to the *Conversion of Saul*, which is seen in direct, natural sunlight, the *Crucifixion of St. Peter* has little natural light focused on it in the Pauline Chapel. Peter becomes a heroic martyr by being crucified upside down by the Romans. He lifts his head and glares out of the painting as the soldiers attempt to rotate the cross and drop it into the freshly dug hole in the ground. Peter and his facial expression is the focal point of the painting.

Bull believes that Michelangelo's frescoes in the Pauline Chapel illustrate "mankind's dependence for salvation on faith in Christ's power and grace."[74] These were Michelangelo's beliefs, sympathetic to those of the Protestant Reformation. According to Bull, the Council of Trent decreed in 1545 that "man's good deeds, not faith alone, counted for salvation; faith was a necessary but not a sufficient condition."[75] These questions of faith and salvation were very much on Michelangelo's mind in the last years of his life.

Return to Architecture

While working on the paintings in the Pauline Chapel, Michelangelo also took on architectural projects for Paul. He designed and supervised the building of the third story and the cornice (projecting ledge) of the Palazzo Farnese, (the palace of Paul's family). Instead of continuing the classical style of the first two floors, Michelangelo expanded the windows and raised the ceilings in the new Mannerist style. The pope also commissioned the aging Michelangelo to remodel the Campidoglio, the civic center of Rome on the Capitoline Hill. Although the work was planned in the late 1530s to impress the Holy Roman emperor Charles V when he visited Rome, the project was unfinished for many years, though Michelangelo's original design was the basis for much of the remodeling.

The bronze equestrian statue of Emperor Marcus Aurelius was moved to the center of the site, and Michelangelo carved a new pedestal for it. Around the statue, in the central courtyard, he proposed three buildings. New facades were planned for two of the existing buildings, the Palazzo Senatorio, home of the Roman Senate, and the Palazzo Conservatori, seat of the city government. A new building, the Palazzo Nuovo, was designed

*M*ichelangelo worked on his own personal pietà, which historians believe was meant to decorate his own tomb. From one single block of marble, Buonarotti sculpted four figures. According to art history professor Joachim Poeschke in his book *Michelangelo and His World,* the figures were linked "by the heavy, sinking figure of Christ, which is only held upright by the support of the three living figures,"[1] the Virgin Mary, Mary Magdalene, and Nicodemus. "Sculpting four figures in a single block—moreover ones not aligned on the same plane—was a challenge that no Italian sculptor had previously attempted," writes art conservator and Michelangelo expert Antonio Forcellino in his book *Michelangelo: A Tormented Life.* "The figure of Nicodemus is a self-portrait of Michelangelo . . . [who] wished to signify his very deep involvement in the worship of Christ, the instrument of mankind's salvation."[2]

In the late 1550s, depressed over his servant Urbino's death, Pope Paul IV's vendetta against him, and the imprisonment of his friend Cardinal Morone, Michelangelo lost his temper and in a fit of rage, smashed part of the pietà with a heavy hammer. Part of Jesus's left leg, collarbone, and left arm was shattered. Art conservator Forcellino declares, "The sculpture remained permanently mutilated, a symbol of a tormented conscience and an uncontrollable anger. . . . The damage he inflicted on it could be compared to killing

opposite the Palazzo Conservatori to match the new facades of the other buildings.

Michelangelo also created a massive ramped staircase, called the Cordonata, which stretched from the bottom of the hill to the main courtyard at the top of the hill. The steps were gently sloped and built wide to allow horses and carriages to ride up to the top. This staircase was flanked at the bottom by two black granite Egyptian lions and at the top by two large statues of Castor and Pollux, legendary protectors of Rome in the fifth century B.C. The Cordonata and the statue of Marcus one's own offspring."[3] Biographer Giorgio Vasari in *The Life of Michelangelo* writes that there was a defective vein in the marble, and the sculpture was abandoned, but Forcellino believes that rage and misery fueled this outbreak, not a flaw in the marble. Michelangelo gave what remained of the pietà to

his friend Francesco Bandini, who hired another sculptor to repair it, but who was unsuccessful. Today, this piece is exhibited at the Museo dell'Opera del Duomo in Florence.

1. Joachim Poeschke. *Michelangelo and His World: Sculpture of the Italian Renaissance.* New York: Harry N. Abrams, 1992, p. 120.
2. Antonio Forcellino. *Michelangelo: A Tormented Life.* Cambridge: Polity, 2009, pp. 287–288.
3. Forcellino. *Michelangelo: A Tormented Life,* pp. 289–290.

Michelangelo's restored Florentine Pietà. It is thought that the artist destroyed part of it in a fit of rage over the imprisonment of his friend Cardinal Morone.

Aurelius were the only works completed at the time of Michelangelo's death. The Campidoglio design by Michelangelo is considered to be one of the first civic planning projects built around a central monument and was often imitated by architects in later years.

Chief Architect of St. Peter's

The old buildings of St. Peter's Basilica in Rome had deteriorated and were near collapse during Michelangelo's life. The original church, more than a thousand years old, was built in

A.D. 319. by Constantine, the first Christian Roman emperor on the site where St. Peter was buried. The new building, under the supervision of the pope's architect, Antonio da Sangallo the Younger, hardly looked much better. Sangallo died in 1546, and Paul appointed Michelangelo chief architect of St. Peter's in November 1546.

Michelangelo was seventy-one years old and had been very ill in the previous year. Against his will, he bowed to the wishes of the pope and accepted the appointment. Michelangelo wrote to his nephew Lionardo Buonarroti, "Many believe—and I believe—that I have been designated for this work by God. In spite of my old age, I do not want to give it up; I work out of love for God and I put all my hope in Him."[76] St. Peter's became his top priority for the remainder of his life. It was so important that he never again returned to Florence, despite the continued urging of Cosimo de' Medici, the new ruler of the city.

Rebuilding the new basilica had first begun under Pope Julius II with architect Donato Bramante while Michelangelo was hard at work on the Sistine Chapel ceiling. Although Bramante was an excellent designer, he was an average engineer and, as Wallace notes, "seriously impaired the structural integrity of the new church."[77] Bramante died in 1514, and many other architects unsuccessfully attempted to add or improve upon the original design. Over the years, the lack of funds often brought the project to a standstill, and there were accusations of wasteful spending against the papacy. Sangallo became the chief architect in the 1540s, and his plan for the church was very large and dark.

Improvements and Innovations

Michelangelo restored Bramante's original architectural plan for St. Peter's and simplified it. He destroyed most of the construction added on since 1514, despite opposition from competitors. Then he designed the beautiful dome of St. Peter's based on Bramante's original concept and the cathedral dome in Florence, built by Filippo Brunelleschi. Michelangelo focused on the light and included twice as many windows as previous architects had. Forcellino declares that "this use of

light can undoubtedly be explained by Michelangelo's religious feelings, since he interpreted the clear and direct light as the emanation of the divine spirit that calls the faithful to Christ."[78]

Wallace writes, "From ground to lantern, the building rises in one continuous sweep. . . . The solid mass and complex surface of St. Peter's exterior contrasts with the spacious, luminous interior. . . . At the center of the immense building is the grave of Saint Peter, and over this venerated spot soars the majestic, light-filled dome."[79]

The new St. Peter's was completed long after the death of Michelangelo. The great artist, however, ensured the continuation and accurate implementation of his original plans for the structure by on-site supervision of the work and written instructions. "The power of his conception transcends the earthly end of its author," declares Umberto Baldini. "Those who came later could not but follow his indications. . . . Michelangelo's instructions were followed faithfully for decades."[80] According to

Michelangelo's design for the St. Peter's dome focused on the effects of light and included twice as many windows as previous designs had. Shown are exterior and interior views of the structure.

Forcellino, St. Peter's had become a symbol of Michelangelo's mortality and his quest for salvation and redemption by God.

Death of Paul, and a New Pope Is Elected

When Paul died in 1549, Michelangelo lost a friend, admirer, and a great patron. Paul was succeeded by another Buonarroti supporter, Cardinal Giovanni Maria Ciocchi del Monte who took the name of Julius III. The new pope continued to support Michelangelo as chief architect of St. Peter's, defended him from his critics, and sought his thoughts and judgment on any new art projects he considered.

An atmosphere of suspicion and repression grew in Rome under Julius. This environment was encouraged by Cardinal Giampietro Carafa of the Inquisitional Tribunal whose main goal in life was opposing heresy. He rooted out deviation from the church's teachings, in any form, by the arrest, questioning, and even torture of heretics. Carafa criticized the nudity in the *Last Judgment* and challenged Michelangelo's decisions as St. Peter's chief architect, but the esteemed artist was safely under the pope's protection.

Julius died after a sudden illness and fever in 1555. The newly elected pope was Marcello Cervino, who called himself Marcellus II. He supported church reform but died of a stroke after twenty-two days in office. He was succeeded by Carafa who took the name of Paul IV. On the first day of his papacy, he suspended all monetary payments to Michelangelo for his work as chief architect. Cosimo de' Medici tried to bring the famous artist back to Florence and protect him against the pope's reprisals, but Michelangelo would not leave St. Peter's.

Crusade of Extremism

The pope's campaign against heretics bordered on the fanatical. He forced all Jews to live in a Roman ghetto, locking them in at night. He required Jewish men to wear yellow hats, and Jewish women, veils or shawls. The pope declared that all Jews were condemned by God to slavery. He banned and burned books that contained what he considered heresy and impris-

FAME, SADNESS, GRIEF

*M*ichelangelo's worldwide fame protected him from powerful adversaries like Pope Paul IV and others. The seventy-five-year-old was internationally famous in 1550 when Giorgio Vasari's book *Lives of the Artists* was published (which included *The Life of Michelangelo*), and it further enhanced his celebrity. Ascanio Condivi's biography, also called *The Life of Michelangelo,* was printed in 1553 to correct the mistakes of Vasari's book, and a revised edition by Vasari was published in 1568. According to art conservator Antonio Forcellino in his book *Michelangelo: A Tormented Life,* "Michelangelo was now receiving letters from the King of France, Queen Catherine [Caterina de' Medici], Duke Cosimo, and numerous cardinals who approached him with the same manners they would have adopted with their peers."

The mid-1550s were sad years for Michelangelo. The last of his family, Gismondo, his brother, died in 1555. (His older brother Lionardo, the monk, had died in 1510. His other brother Giovansimone had died in 1548. Buonaroto had passed away in 1528, and his father, Ludovico, died in 1531). Buonaroto's children were Michelangelo's only heirs, and several died in childhood. His main beneficiary was his nephew Lionardo, who still resided in Florence. Michelangelo's friend and longtime household assistant, Urbino, died in 1555. Urbino's wife, Cornelia, and young son, also named Michelangelo, lived in Michelangelo's household with him while Urbino was alive. They soon left, but Michelangelo was never alone. In addition to a male assistant, he employed one or two female housekeepers at all times.

Antonio Forcellino. *Michelangelo: A Tormented Life.* Cambridge: Polity, 2009, p. 278.

oned Cardinal Giovanni Morone, Michelangelo's close friend and spiritual adviser. The work at St. Peter's came almost completely to a halt, although the pope did not change any of Michelangelo's designs. Vasari notes that the pope was in favor of covering the private parts of figures in the *Last Judgment* and the nudity of angels in the *Conversion of St. Paul* and *Crucifixion of St. Peter*. Under Paul IV's papacy, Michelangelo's earnings were reduced to a trickle.

In the late 1550s Michelangelo designed a church in Rome for Florentine exiles who resided in the city—San Giovanni dei Fiorentini. In 1557 the aged artist actually left Rome for a short time when he thought the Spanish troops in Naples were about to occupy the Holy City. That never happened, since a settlement was reached, but Michelangelo fled to the mountains of Spoleto and enjoyed a brief stay in the countryside.

In 1564 Michelangelo completed his final architectural project, the restoration of the Porta Pia, a gate in Rome.

A Kinder, Gentler Pope

The turbulent reign of Paul IV finally ended with his death in 1559. The new pope, Pius IV, was Cardinal Giovanni Angelo de' Medici of Milan, a patron of the arts as were his distant Medici cousins in Florence. Pius was less harsh and violent than his unpopular predecessor, restored part of Michelangelo's pension, and again gave the eighty-four-year-old artist complete control over St. Peter's.

Under Pius, Michelangelo was extremely busy despite failing eyesight and other medical conditions, including kidney stones. He worked on designs for the Sforza Chapel at the Basilica di Santa Maria Maggiore in Rome and a restoration of the Church of Santa Maria degli Angeli, also in Rome. His last architectural project, in 1561, was the renovation of the city gate known as the Porta Pia and the surrounding area of the city, which was completed in 1564. He continued to sculpt and draw in his own workshop until his final days.

As Michelangelo headed into extreme old age, his original family and most of his friends were already dead. His thoughts turned to death, to Jesus Christ and religious study, and to his own life and personal salvation.

6

Questions of Spirituality, Love, and Death: The Last Days

The last years of Michelangelo were filled with personal thoughts and beliefs about religious doctrine and spirituality. He focused on his imminent death and whether he would obtain salvation. These issues were linked with two significant loving relationships in his life, apart from his family. One was with a woman, Vittoria Colonna, while the other was with a man, Tommaso de' Cavalieri. These associations examined aspects of his devoutness as well as his sexuality and how it influenced his art.

Vittoria Colonna

Fifteen years younger than Michelangelo, Colonna came from a powerful and noble family of Rome that strongly supported Charles V, the Holy Roman emperor. At the age of nineteen, she married the Marquess of Pescara, Ferrante Francesco d'Avalos, who helped the emperor's troops win a victory against the French king in 1525, then died shortly after of battle wounds. A widow at the age of thirty-five, she became well known in her own right as an excellent poet and she socialized in the very best literary circles. This was likely how she met Michelangelo, who also wrote poetry and was already famous for his artwork. Both also shared a devotion to religion, and they became close friends. It is believed that Michelangelo gave her drawings of the *Crucifixion* and the *Pietà*. William E. Wallace writes, "Drawings and poems poured forth from the artist. He was the eager admirer; she the appreciative but slightly more restrained recipient of ardent affections. They spent time in each other's company."[81]

Vittoria Colonna was a close friend of Michelangelo, and he wrote many poems to her about love, art, religion, and beauty.

Michelangelo wrote many poems to Colonna. He wrote to her about love, art, beauty, and religion. The following sonnet was written in 1550:

> When divine Art conceives a form and face,
> She bids the craftsman for his first essay
> To shape a simple model in mere clay:
> This is the earliest birth of Art's embrace.
> From the live marble in the second place
> His mallet brings into the light of day
> A thing so beautiful that who can say
> When time shall conquer that immortal grace?
> Thus my own model I was born to be—
> The model of that nobler self, whereto
> Schooled by your pity, lady, I shall grow.
> Each overplus and each deficiency
> You will make good. What penance then is due
> For my fierce heat, chastened and taught by you?[82]

The Spirituals

Colonna, Michelangelo, and several others formed a group that met regularly to debate and discuss issues of religious reform and spirituality in light of the Protestant Reformation in Europe. Antonio Forcellino writes that the gathering, often referred to as the Spirituals, met secretly and talked about things like divine grace, the logic of the scriptures, and even the existence of heaven and hell. English cardinal Reginald Pole was one of the Spirituals, as well as Cardinal Giovanni Marone, Michelangelo's religious mentor, who was later imprisoned by Pope Paul IV for heresy.

The group supported reform to resolve the crisis of the Counter-Reformation and reconcile the church with the Lutherans. They discussed the possibility that salvation was obtained by faith and not good works, and that the church need not be mediators between God and humans. They questioned the absolute authority of the pope and the celibacy of the priests. These unorthodox ideas undermined the power of the church in Rome, and members of the Spirituals were harassed or persecuted as heretics. The pope, however, was willing to overlook Michelangelo because of his fame and artistic talent. Pole returned to England in 1551, and the Spirituals soon disbanded.

In Mourning

Colonna died in Rome in 1547, and her death was a terrible blow to Michelangelo. Together they had reached a unique spiritual awareness, and Michelangelo depended on her for affection and support, and as a companion who also struggled with her religious beliefs.

ALL IN THE FAMILY

*M*ichelangelo took family responsibility very seriously and supported his brother Buonaroto's two surviving children, Francesca and Lionardo. He provided the dowry [a wedding gift of money] when Francesca married in 1537 and advised Lionardo, who was his only male heir, when it was time to take a wife.

Lionardo and Michelangelo exchanged letters frequently and grew very close. The nephew often sent his uncle articles of clothing, wine, and food to be sure he dressed and ate well. When Michelangelo became ill on several occasions, Lionardo hurried to Rome to be with his uncle. The great artist survived and each time berated his nephew that he only visited to preserve his inheritance.

It took eight years to find Lionardo a suitable wife from a noble family with a sizable dowry. Finally Lionardo married Cassandra di Donato Ridolfi in 1553. Michelangelo gave her expensive jewelry as a wedding gift. Cassandra gave birth to a son in April 1554. They named him Buonarroto. Lionardo and his wife had several more children, including another son they named Michelangelo, but most were born after the aging artist's death. He did, however, get to know his grandnephew, who guaranteed a continuation of the family line. Young Buonarroto Buonarroti was ten when his famous great-uncle died.

Michelangelo wrote several sonnets in response to her death. They dealt with the aging artist's love and grief and the certainty of death. In "To Vittoria Colonna," Michelangelo proclaims:

When she who was the cause of all my sighs,
Departed from the world, herself, and me,
Nature, who fain had made us worthy her,
Rested ashamed, and who had seen her wept.
But let not boastful Death, who quenched the light
Of this our sun of suns, be all too vain;
Since love hath conquered him, and let her live,
Both here on earth and 'mong the saints above.
It seemed a cruel and unrighteous thing
For Death to make her scattered virtues dumb,
And bear her soul where it might show less fair.
But (contradiction strange!) her writings now
Make her more living than she was in life;
And heaven receives her dead, where she had else no part.[83]

Tommaso de' Cavalieri

Whereas the relationship between Michelangelo and Vittoria Colonna was strictly a platonic and spiritual bonding, historians are uncertain as to the exact relationship between the aging artist and the handsome young Cavalieri. When the two first met, Michelangelo, a known admirer of the male body on canvas, was struck by Cavalieri's physical beauty and seemed instantly infatuated. They exchanged letters discussing their fondness and respect for each other, and Michelangelo gave him several drawings as gifts.

According to Antonio Forcellini,

The three drawings . . . all depict subjects that allude to the torments of love: Phaethon falling from the sky for having dared to come too close to the sun, a metaphor for the presumption of which Michelangelo felt guilty for having approached young Tommaso, himself a "sun"; Tityus tormented by Zeus' eagle for having stolen fire from the gods, and chained to a rock like a lover to his loved one; and the abduction of Ganymede by Zeus' eagle, which was a metaphor for the soul raised up to the heavens by the sentiment of love.[84]

Luciano Berti, director of the galleries and San Marco Museum in Florence, writes in *The Complete Work of Michelangelo* that "In point of fact these drawings are nothing more nor less than equivalents of love poems, in which the eros [love] is manifested and at the same time holds itself back . . . while betraying a dark background of remorse and conflict."[85]

The letters and sonnets exchanged between the two men should be read in light of sixteenth-century mores, when older men advised younger men as their mentors, and mutually exchanged impassioned letters or sonnets of love and friendship that were considered socially acceptable at the time. In one letter, Michelangelo wrote to Cavalieri, "I could sooner forget the food on which I live, which unhappily nourishes only the body, than your name, which nourishes body and soul, filling

Vittoria Colonna's book of Michelangelo's poems he gave her. Michelangelo wrote poetry to many people, including the young Tommaso de' Cavalieri.

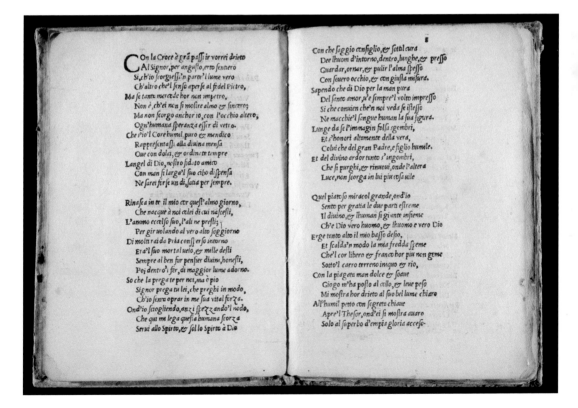

both with such delight that I am insensible to sorrow or fear of death, while my memory of you endures."[86]

In a sonnet thought to be dedicated to Cavalieri, Michelangelo writes:

Through your clear eyes I view a beauteous light,
That my dark sight would ever seek in vain;
With your firm steps a burden I support,
Which my weak power was never used to bear
I soar aloft, unplumed, upon your wings,
By your intelligence to heaven am raised;
Your smile or frown maketh me pale or red,
Cold in the sun, warm 'mid severest chills.
In your will is mine own will ever fixed;
My thoughts find birth and growth within your heart;
My words are from your spirit only drawn;
And like the moon, alone in heaven, I seem,
That to our eyes were indiscernible,
Save by that light which from the sun proceeds.[87]

Cavalieri remained a good friend to Michelangelo for nearly thirty years. He was there with him when the great artist died in Rome in 1564.

Sexuality and Michelangelo's Art

The question of Michelangelo's sexuality and how it influenced his art remains in the realm of speculation by art historians who have no actual proof one way or the other. James Beck believes that "it is most likely that his sexual experiences . . . were minimal—and possibly even nonexistent."[88] Regarding abstinence, Michelangelo once said, "I have always practiced it. If you wish to prolong your life, restrain yourself as much as you can."[89] He believed that abstinence kept a person young, and he guided his passion and enthusiasm into his works of art. His love for Colonna and Cavalieri inspired him, resulting in an outpouring of artwork and writing.

Beck notes that Michelangelo may possibly have had a fear of women and an aversion to physical love. Another factor leading to abstinence may have been that venereal disease, especially

Il Crepusculo, or *Twilight,* was sketched in chalk. Michelangelo admired the beauty of the human body, whether in male or female form.

syphilis, was widespread in Italy and Europe during the artist's lifetime. There was no cure at the time, and many died a difficult death, covered in sores and boils. Homosexual behavior was strictly outlawed, and punishment was severe. Beck concludes, "The skimpy evidence that survives suggests that Michelangelo— whether through disinclination, restraint, shyness, conviction, or fear—held his libido in check and that he had few, if any, sexual experiences."[90]

Ascanio Condivi writes that Michelangelo admired and loved the human body and all beautiful things. Since he painted mainly male nudes, some in the sixteenth century openly questioned his sexuality. Michelangelo asked, "Whose judgment would be so barbarous as not to appreciate that the foot of a man is more noble than his boot, and his skin more noble than that of a sheep, with which he is dressed?"[91] Beck declares, "The fact that he admired and rendered marvelous images of young men cannot be used as evidence of latent or real homosexuality, nor, for that matter, can the masculation of his woman subjects." Beck continues, "Michelangelo did not use female models and never drew a nude woman from life, basing his renderings on males, usually his studio boys, as was customary."[92]

A Different Viewpoint

Forcellino has a different opinion. He believes that Michelangelo was tormented by his repressed sexuality, among other things. In his biography *Michelangelo: A Tormented Life* Forcellino writes, "There can be no doubt that Michelangelo suffered from his tortured and turbulent personality, his repressed or at least never happily experienced homosexuality, and his diffidence, which transformed into a persecution complex on encountering the least problem." Forcellino notes that he was "in a state of continuous guilt,"[93] and that is why he was always concerned about his salvation and redemption, because despite being a devoutly religious man, he knew he was a sinner like every other person.

Michelangelo publicly admitted he was a platonic lover of men and considered it the highest form of friendship, as did many others in Renaissance Italy. This spiritual, nonphysical type of love inspired many of his masterpieces.

The Rondandini *Pietà*

According to Wallace, Michelangelo in his last years, "now carved for his health and the salvation of his soul. . . . It seems that carving was a form of prayer, a way of bringing himself closer to God. Salvation through creation."[94]

Michelangelo worked on the *Rondandini Pietà* until six days before he died. It was 6 feet 6⅜ inches (1.94m) high and consisted of just the two standing figures of Christ and Mary, which seemingly merged into one another. Lutz Heusinger talks about "the unity between Mother and Son" and writes, "It is almost impossible to tell whether it is the Mother supporting the Son, or the Son supporting the Mother, overcome by despair. Both are in need of help, and both hold themselves up in the act of invocation and lament before the world and God."[95] This pietà was likely sculpted for Michelangelo's own tomb. The artist destroyed his first version, and in the second unfinished pietà there is an arm in mid-air, writes Wallace, that "is a ghostly remnant of an earlier composition."[96]

Michelangelo also worked on a series of drawings of the Crucifixion as if, according to Wallace, he was in physical contact with God. In his art and his poetry, he focused on the theme of death and sorrow, and put words to paper as he sculpted or sketched:

Ah, woe is me! Alas! When I revolve
My years gone by, wearied, I find not one
Wherein to call a single day my own.
Fallacious hopes, desires as vain, and thoughts
Of love compounded and of lover's woes
(No mortal joy has novelty for me),
Make up the sum; I know, I feel, 't is so.
Thus have I ever strayed from Truth and Good:
Where'er I go, shifting from right to left,
Denser the shades, less bright the sun appears,
And I, infirm and worn, am nigh to fall.[97]

At Long Last, the End

By the end of 1663 the cold, rainy weather aggravated the nearly eighty-nine-year-old artist's physical condition, causing weakness in his limbs and sleepiness. When awake, Michelangelo was still sharp and lucid, but his condition deteriorated to the point where his friend, Daniele Ricciarelli da Volterra, wrote Michelangelo's only heir and nephew, Lionardo, to come to Rome.

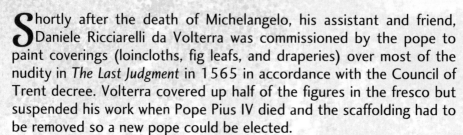

COVER-UP

Shortly after the death of Michelangelo, his assistant and friend, Daniele Ricciarelli da Volterra was commissioned by the pope to paint coverings (loincloths, fig leafs, and draperies) over most of the nudity in *The Last Judgment* in 1565 in accordance with the Council of Trent decree. Volterra covered up half of the figures in the fresco but suspended his work when Pope Pius IV died and the scaffolding had to be removed so a new pope could be elected.

According to the website of the Uffizi Gallery in Florence, Volterra became "infamously known as Il Braghettone, which means the breeches-maker," although he was a fine artist in his own right who completed a bronze bust of Michelangelo as well as numerous paintings. Volterra lived and worked in Michelangelo's house until his own death at fifty-nine in 1566.

Pope Pius V succeeded Pius IV and actually considered destroying all classical antiquities in Rome like the Colosseum and arches throughout the city, in addition to classical statues that were collected privately or displayed in public. The pope considered this because he regarded the artwork in question to be pagan, which diverted visitors' attention away from St. Peter's and the other beautiful Roman churches. Fortunately for all of posterity, the pope decided against such action.

Uffizi Gallery. "Daniele Ricciarelli da Volterra Biography." www.virtualuffizi.com/biography/Daniele -Ricciarelli-da-Volterra.htm.

After a carving session on the *Rondandini Pietà*, Michelangelo began feeling feverish and sick. He ordered his drawings, sketches, and cartoons burned "in order," writes Giorgio Vasari, "that no one should perceive his labours and the efforts of his genius, that he might not appear less than perfect."[98] He became worse, and with his physician and friends (including Cavalieri) gathered around him, he declared his will out loud, "leaving his soul to God, his body to the earth, and his property to his nearest relations,"[99] states Vasari.

Michelangelo passed away on February 18, 1564, less than three weeks before his eighty-ninth birthday. Of the works found in his house, most were cartoons. All were of religious topics. Beck believes that Michelangelo may have had his own bonfire of the vanities, as did the Florence priest Savonarola so many years before. "He gathered together his much-guarded drawings and cartoons, over which he had been especially secretive, and set them to flames. Could some have been too pagan or sexually explicit?" asks Beck. "We shall never know."[100] Both the church and Duke Cosimo of Florence were extremely disappointed that the famed artist had not left behind any finished paintings or sculpture. The *Rondanini Pietà* and what cartoons remained were seized by church officials. A sealed box that contained eight thousand gold ducats was left for Lionardo.

Homeward Bound

Forcellino summarizes the inventory of what was found in Michelangelo's house on the morning after his death: "A few 'threadbare' items of clothing, 'an iron bedstead with sack of straw, three mattresses, two white woolen blankets and one of white lambskin' . . . no piece of furniture of any value, no pictures and no precious objects." Forcellino writes, "But one by one, they pulled out dented copper vases, chipped ceramic ones, knotted handkerchiefs and worn sacks. . . . The notary searched the house . . . for precious furnishings, mirrors, silverware, gold-plate, damasks and oriental silk. But he found none of this—none of what you would have expected to find in the house of any affluent man in Rome."[101]

The pope wanted the body to be buried in Rome, but Michelangelo had expressed a wish several days before his death to be buried in Florence. Leonardo, who arrived in Rome three days after his uncle died, secretly and with Cosimo's help, wrapped up Michelangelo's corpse and, according to Vasari, "removed the body from Rome and forwarded it to Florence like merchandise."[102] The cold weather preserved the remains that arrived in Florence on March 11. The Medicis helped to prepare an elaborate funeral and the creation of a tomb in the

SISTINE CHAPEL RESTORATION

In 1980 work began on the restoration of the Sistine Chapel frescoes by Michelangelo. A team of restorers and art historians was formed by Vatican officials. Their goal was to remove all soot, grime, dirt, and candle wax smoke that had caused discoloration, as well as to repair cracks and damage caused by water seepage and salt deposits over hundreds of years. The team also removed any previous repainting, oil, or varnish. Several restorations had been carried out in the past (in 1625, 1710–1713, 1935–1938), including the application of a wine mixture to clean the frescoes, glue-varnish to refresh the colors, and the repainting of certain areas. The Nippon Television Network Corporation of Japan paid $4.2 million to film every stage of the restoration, which was completed in December 1999.

The first stage involved the construction of aluminum scaffolding, and the team used the same holes in the walls that Michelangelo had used for his wooden scaffolding five hundred years earlier. The effect of the restoration was an overall lightening of the frescoes and a brightening of colors. All windows were closed to protect the masterpieces from automobile exhaust, dust, dirt, and humidity. An air conditioning system and air filtration unit were installed to keep the temperature constant at all times, between 68°F (20°C) in the summer and 77°F (25°C) in the winter.

In a project beginning in 1980 and completed in 1999 the Sistine Chapel was restored to its original luster. A Japanese film crew filmed the entire restoration for $4.2 million.

Buonarroti family church at Santa Croce. Many thousands came out for the memorial service in his honor.

Michelangelo had finally come home to Florence.

His Legacy

When young Michelangelo Buonarroti decided to become an artist, it was considered a lower-class position similar to a workman or craftsman, beneath the status of a noble family from Florence. The life of Michelangelo changed that commonly held belief. He elevated the title and position of artist and sculptor in society and accumulated much wealth and great status. He became world famous and achieved great respect and celebrity. His friends were kings, popes, noblemen, and cardinals, and they all clamored for a work of art by the great artist.

Wallace declares,

> Few artists have achieved as much as Michelangelo in such diverse fields of endeavor; few so completely embody the notion of artistic genius. However, his legacy is greater than the sum of his works. More than any of his contemporaries, he significantly raised the stature of his profession, from craftsman to genius, from artisan to gentleman. He demanded respect from his patrons, and he earned prestige as an artist.[103]

Michelangelo influenced other artists and their creative styles, both when he lived and long after his death. His unforgettable works continue to thrill and amaze millions of people who have flocked to Rome and Florence over the centuries to see his enduring masterpieces.

Notes

Introduction: A Life of Troubled Brilliance

1. Giorgio Vasari. *The Life of Michelangelo.* Translated by A.B. Hinds. London: Pallas Athene, 2006, p. 5. (First published in Florence in 1550, this translation by A.B. Hinds is based on the text of the second edition of 1568.)
2. Jayne Pettit. *Michelangelo: Genius of the Renaissance.* New York: Franklin Watts, 1998, p. 11.
3. William E. Wallace. *Michelangelo: The Artist, the Man, and His Times.* New York: Cambridge University Press, 2010, p. 340.
4. Vasari. *The Life of Michelangelo*, pp. 35, 210.
5. Vasari. *The Life of Michelangelo*, p. 200.
6. Antonio Forcellino. *Michelangelo: A Tormented Life.* Cambridge: Polity, 2009, pp. 5, 10.
7. Quoted in Vasari. *The Life of Michelangelo*, p. 207.

Chapter 1: Early Years: The Developing Artist

8. Ascanio Condivi. *The Life of Michelangelo.* Translated by C.B. Holroyd. London: Pallas Athene, 2006, p. 40.

9. Quoted in Vasari. *The Life of Michelangelo*, p. 36.
10. George Bull. *Michelangelo: A Biography.* New York: St. Martin's, 1995, p. 9.
11. Wallace. *Michelangelo*, p. 32.
12. Ross King. *Michelangelo & the Pope's Ceiling.* New York: Walker, 2003, p. 73.
13. Condivi. *The Life of Michelangelo*, p. 41.
14. Forcellino. *Michelangelo*, p. 21.
15. Bull. *Michelangelo*, p. 21.
16. John T. Spike. *Young Michelangelo: The Path to the Sistine.* New York: Vendome, 2010, p. 55.
17. James Beck. *Three Worlds of Michelangelo.* New York: W.W. Norton, 1999, p. 67.
18. Condivi. *The Life of Michelangelo*, pp. 49–50.
19. Condivi. *The Life of Michelangelo*, p. 157.
20. Forcellino. *Michelangelo: A Tormented Life*, p. 38.

Chapter 2: The Young Genius in Rome and Florence

21. Spike. *Young Michelangelo: The Path to the Sistine*, p. 97.

22. Condivi. *The Life of Michelangelo*, pp. 62, 64.

23. Vasari. *The Life of Michelangelo*, p. 52.

24. Quoted in Spike. *Young Michelangelo: The Path to the Sistine*, pp. 109–110.

25. Condivi. *The Life of Michelangelo*, p. 65.

26. Joachim Poeschke. *Michelangelo and His World: Sculpture of the Italian Renaissance.* New York: Harry N. Abrams, 1992, p. 75.

27. Wallace. *Michelangelo*, p. 23.

28. Spike. *Young Michelangelo*, p. 126.

29. Quoted in Spike. *Young Michelangelo*, pp. 126–127.

30. Umberto Baldini. "Sculpture." In *The Complete Work of Michelangelo.* Novara, Italy: Barnes & Noble by arrangement with Orbis, 1996, p. 104.

31. Poeschke. *Michelangelo and His Work*, p. 86.

32. Condivi. *The Life of Michelangelo*, p. 70.

33. Vasari. *The Life of Michelangelo*, p. 59.

34. Wallace. *Michelangelo*, p. 60.

35. Forcellino. *Michelangelo*, p. 64.

36. Wallace. *Michelangelo*, p. 70.

37. Beck. *Three Worlds of Michelangelo*, p. 142.

38. Vasari. *The Life of Michelangelo*, p. 62.

Chapter 3: Head to Head with the Pope: The Sistine Chapel

39. Lutz Heusinger. *Michelangelo: Life and Works.* Rome: Edizioni d'Arte, 1982, p. 16.

40. Condivi. *The Life of Michelangelo*, p. 80.

41. King. *Michelangelo & the Pope's Ceiling*, pp. 53–54.

42. King. *Michelangelo & the Pope's Ceiling*, p. 245.

43. King. *Michelangelo & the Pope's Ceiling*, p. 266.

44. Bull. *Michelangelo: A Biography*, p. 99.

45. Quoted in Ednah D. Cheney. *Selected Poems from Michelangelo Buonarroti.* Trans. John Addington Symonds. Boston: Lee and Shepard, 1885, p. 61. Historical reproduction. Charleston, SC: BiblioLife, 2009.

46. Quoted in Condivi. *The Life of Michelangelo*, p. 104.

47. Vasari. *The Life of Michelangelo*, pp. 94, 96.

48. Quoted in Bull. *Michelangelo: A Biography*, p.104.

49. Quoted in King. *Michelangelo & the Pope's Ceiling*, p. 291.

50. Quoted in Wallace. *Michelangelo*, p. 105.

51. Forcellino. *Michelangelo*, p. 110.

52. Poeschke. *Michelangelo and His World*, p. 96.

53. Baldini. "Sculpture." *The Complete Work of Michelangelo*, p. 115.

Chapter 4: Florence and the Medicis: In and Out of Power

54. Bull. *Michelangelo*, p. 133.

55. Vasari. *The Life of Michelangelo*, pp. 100–101.

56. Quoted in Bull. *Michelangelo*, pp. 140–141.
57. Bull. *Michelangelo*, p. 142.
58. Wallace. *Michelangelo*, p. 121.
59. Quoted in Wallace. *Michelangelo*, p. 145.
60. Wallace. *Michelangelo*, p. 149–150.
61. Wallace. *Michelangelo*, p. 151.
62. Wallace. *Michelangelo*, p. 152.
63. Wallace. *Michelangelo*, p. 154.
64. Bull. *Michelangelo*, p. 215.
65. In Cheney. *Selected Poems from Michelangelo Buonarroti*, p. 139.
66. Poeschke. *Michelangelo and His Work*, p. 67.

Chapter 5: Nel Frattempo di Nuovo a Roma . . . Meanwhile, Back in Rome . . . The Last Judgment

67. Wallace. *Michelangelo*, p. 183.
68. Wallace. *Michelangelo*, p. 183.
69. Forcellino. *Michelangelo*, p. 193.
70. Wallace. *Michelangelo*, p. 185.
71. Vasari. *The Life of Michelangelo*, p. 125.
72. Forcellino. *Michelangelo*, pp. 194–195.
73. Wallace. *Michelangelo*, pp. 251-252.
74. Bull. *Michelangelo*, p. 329.
75. Bull. *Michelangelo*, p. 329.
76. Quoted in Sean Connelly. *Michelangelo*. Milwaukee: Gareth Stevens, World Almanac Library, 2004, p. 40.
77. Wallace. *Michelangelo*, p. 224.
78. Forcellino. *Michelangelo*, p. 275.
79. Wallace. *Michelangelo*, p. 228.
80. Baldini. "Sculpture." *The Complete Work of Michelangelo*, p. 350.

Chapter 6: Questions of Spirituality, Love, and Death: The Last Days

81. Wallace. *Michelangelo*, p. 213.
82. Quoted in Cheney. *Selected Poems from Michelangelo Buonarroti*, p. 67.
83. Cheney. *Selected Poems from Michelangelo Buonarroti*, p. 115.
84. Forcellino. *Michelangelo*, pp. 187–188.
85. Luciano Berti. "Drawings," In *The Complete Work of Michelangelo*. Novara, Italy: Barnes & Noble by arrangement with Orbis, 1996, p. 452.
86. Quoted in Wallace. *Michelangelo*, p. 179.
87. Quoted in Cheney. *Selected Poems from Michelangelo Buonarroti*, p. 85.
88. Beck. *Three Worlds of Michelangelo*, p. 143.
89. Quoted in Beck. *Three Worlds of Michelangelo*, p. 147.
90. Beck. *Three Worlds of Michelangelo*, p. 150.
91. Quoted in Beck. *Three Worlds of Michelangelo*, pp. 151–152.
92. Beck. *Three Worlds of Michelangelo*, p. 152.
93. Forcellino. *Michelangelo*, p. 206.
94. Wallace. *Michelangelo*, p. 321.
95. Heusinger. *Michelangelo*, pp. 31–32.
96. Wallace. *Michelangelo*, p. 321.

97. Quoted in Cheney. *Selected Poems from Michelangelo Buonarroti*, p. 135.
98. Vasari. *The Life of Michelangelo*, p. 194.
99. Vasari. *The Life of Michelangelo*, p. 192.
100. Beck. *Three Worlds of Michelangelo*, p. 231.
101. Forcellino. *Michelangelo*, p. 294.
102. Vasari. *The Life of Michelangelo*, p. 217.
103. Wallace. *Michelangelo*, p. 340.

abstinence: Voluntarily refraining from some indulgence, such as alcohol or sex; self-discipline.

apex: Peak, highpoint.

ardent: Enthusiastic, eager, devoted.

bull: Formal proclamation or order issued by the pope.

cartoon: A full-size preliminary drawing for a fresco painting or other work of art.

celibacy: State of being unmarried and observing abstinence.

classical: Art style of ancient Greece or Rome that emphasizes balance, form, symmetry.

commission: A signed contract with details of work to be produced.

conservator: Restorer of paintings and other artwork.

cornice: Projecting molded feature in architecture.

damask: Fine linen fabric.

devoutness: Devoted to religion, serious, pious.

diffidence: Shyness, reserve, timidity.

discerning: Selective, distinguishing, perceptive.

dowry: A wedding gift of money; payment.

emanation: Something coming from a source.

eros: Love, desire.

facade: The front part of the building.

filial: Referring to a son or daughter; child to a parent.

flayed: Skinned.

fluted: Long, rounded grooves on a column.

fraternal: Referring to brothers; brotherly.

fresco: A method of applying paint directly onto the wet plaster of a wall or ceiling before it dries.

heresy: Dissent or deviation from church teachings.

heretic: Person who practices heresy.

ignudi: Term created by Michelangelo to refer to male nudes on the Sistine Chapel ceiling.

impetuosity: Recklessness.

indulgences: In Catholicism, partial decrease of punishment that is due for sin after forgiveness (absolution).

invocation: Prayer, request, appeal.

latent: Hidden, underlying, suppressed.

liberality: Generosity, bountiousness, open-mindedness.

libido: Sex drive.

lunette: A half-moon, crescent-shaped, semicircular space in architecture.

Mannerism: Art style of the late Renaissance that differed from classical forms, with exaggerated distortions and twists of the human form.

martyr: A person who dies for the sake of a belief or principle.

metaphor: Figure of speech to suggest likeness, symbol, comparison.

mores: Standards, customs, values.

mortality: Death, humanity.

niches: Recession in a wall; cubbyhole.

obscenity: Tastelessness, vulgarity, crudeness.

patron: A person or group that financially supports a person or group to complete a task or job.

pendentive: Triangular-shaped space in corners, where ceiling meets walls.

perspective: The way objects appear to the eye in respect to their distance, depth, and space.

Pietà: Work of art of the Virgin Mary and the dead body of Christ.

pious: Devout, religious, self-righteous.

platonic: Spiritual, nonphysical.

pontificate: A pope's term of office.

posterity: Future generations, descendants.

quarry: Excavation, pit.

Reformation: Religious movement that tried to reform the Catholic Church but resulted in the formation of the Protestant Church.

Renaissance: Rebirth and revival of art, architecture, and learning in fourteenth- and fifteenth-century Italy, using the classical styles of ancient Greece and Rome.

resurrection: In Christian tradition, the rising to life of all the dead before God's final judgment.

sacraments: Ceremonies and rituals such as baptism.

sacristy: Room in a church where robes, garments, sacred vessels, and church treasures are kept, behind or off to the side of the altar.

salvation: The saving of a person from the consequences of a sinful life.

sarcophagus: A large case or box that holds a coffin.

secular: Worldly, earthly.

spandrel: Triangular space between two arches and the molding or ornament above.

spirituality: Holiness, devoutness.

sybils: Wise women who can foretell the future.

tempera: Permanent, fast-drying paint (before oil paints were used) consisting of colored pigment and egg yolk for binding.

theses: Ideas, theories, propositions.

unorthodox: Unconventional, nonconformist, heretical.

vendetta: Dispute, grudge, retaliation.

venerate: Worship, honor, respect.

Important Dates

1475
Michelangelo Buonarroti is born in Caprese, outside of Florence, Italy.

1481
Michelangelo's mother, Francesca, dies on December 6, when he is six years old.

1488
Michelangelo works as an apprentice in Domenico Ghirlandaio's workshop.

1490
Michelangelo studies sculpture at the Medici garden and soon after moves into the Medici household.

1492
Lorenzo de' Medici dies on April 8.

1494
Michelangelo goes to Venice, then to Bologna for a year.

Medicis give up power, leave Florence, and are replaced by republican government.

1496
After a few months in Florence, Michelangelo moves to Rome; begins work on *Bacchus*.

1498–1500
Michelangelo carves *Pietà* and achieves fame and wealth.

1501–1504
Michelangelo returns to Florence and is soon at work on the *David*, another masterpiece.

1503
Pope Alexander VI dies and is succeeded by Pope Pius III, who dies twenty-six days later and is succeeded by Julius II on November 1.

1504
Michelangelo works on the cartoon for the *Battle of Cascina*.

1505
Michelangelo is summoned to Rome by Pope Julius II to carve his tomb.

1506
Michelangelo returns to Florence after argument with the pope about funds for tomb; reconciles with Julius in Bologna.

1507
Michelangelo agrees to work on large bronze statue of Julius.

1508

Michelangelo completes bronze statue in February and returns to Rome in March. After working on the tomb for a short time, Michelangelo begins preliminary work on Sistine Chapel ceiling.

1510

First half of ceiling is completed and uncovered for public.

1511

Bronze statue of Pope Julius II is destroyed by a mob in Bologna.

1512

Michelangelo completes Sistine Chapel ceiling. It is unveiled on October 31.

1513

Pope Julius II dies in Rome in February; Cardinal Giovanni de' Medici becomes pope on March 25 and takes the name Leo X; Medicis regain control of Florentine government.

1516

Pope Leo X commissions Michelangelo to work on facade of San Lorenzo Church in Florence.

1520

Facade project cancelled by pope; Medici family offers Michelangelo commission for family tomb and library.

1521

Pope Leo dies suddenly on December 1; new pope is Adrian IV, who stops Michelangelo's work on Medici tomb and Laurentian Library; Michelangelo goes back to working on tomb of Julius; France joins with England, Venice, Milan, Florence, and the pope to oppose Charles V, the Holy Roman emperor, for control of Italy.

1523

Pope Adrian IV dies unexpectedly in September; new pope is Cardinal Giulio de' Medici, who takes the name of Clement VII; Clement puts Michelangelo back to work on Medici tomb and Laurentian Library; War continues against imperial forces of Holy Roman emperor.

1527

Siege of Rome begins on May 6; Pope Clement is held prisoner for seven months; Florence expels Medicis and establishes another republic.

1528

Michelangelo cuts back on Medici projects and directs Florences fortifications against imperial forces; siege of Florence; death of Michelangelo's brother, Buonarroto Buonarroti.

1530

Pope publicly crowns Charles as Holy Roman emperor in February; Medicis restored to power in Florence.

1531

Ludovico Buonarroti, father of Michelangelo, dies in Florence.

1532

Michelangelo meets Tommaso de Cavalieri.

1534

Pope Clement dies and is succeeded by Pope Paul III; Michelangelo stops work on all Medici projects, leaves Florence and moves to Rome; begins preliminary work on the *Last Judgment*.

1538

Michelangelo meets Vittoria Colonna; designs the Piazza del Campidoglio (Capitoline Hill) in Rome.

1541

Michelangelo completes fresco of the *Last Judgment*; it is unveiled to the public on December 25.

1542–1550

Michelangelo works on frescoes of *Conversion of Saul* and *Crucifixion of St. Peter*.

1545

The completed tomb of Julius II is unveiled at Church of San Pietro in Rome.

1546

Pope names Michelangelo chief architect of St. Peter's in November.

1548

Michelangelo's brother Giovansimone Buonarroti dies.

1549

Pope Paul dies; he is succeeded by Pope Julius III.

1550

Giorgio Vasari publishes biography of Michelangelo in *Lives of the Artists*.

1553

Ascanio Condivi publishes biography of Michelangelo; Michelangelo's nephew Lionardo Buonarroti marries Cassandra di Donato Ridolfi.

1554

Cassandra gives birth to a son, who is named Buonarroto, and the Buonarroti family name is extended.

1555

Pope Julius dies and is succeeded by Pope Marcellus II, who dies after twenty-two days and is succeeded by Pope Paul IV; Michelangelo's brother Gismondo dies, leaving the great artist as the last surviving member of the original Buonarroti family.

Michelangelo's beloved assistant Urbino dies.

1559

Pope Paul IV dies and is succeeded by Pope Pius IV; Michelangelo designs the San Giovanni dei Fiorentini Church in Rome.

1560

Michelangelo designs Sforza Chapel in Santa Maria Maggiore in Rome.

1561

Michelangelo works on restoration of Church of Santa Maria degli Angeli in Rome; begins renovation of Porta Pia in Rome.

1564
Michelangelo dies on February 18.

1565
Cover-up of the nude figures in Michelangelo's *Last Judgement*.

1980
Work begins on modern restoration of the Sistine Chapel frescoes.

1999
Sistine Chapel fresco restorations are completed.

For More Information

Books

Hugo Chapman. *Michelangelo*. New Haven, CT: Yale University Press, 2006. This book focuses on the sketches and drawings of Michelangelo in which his ideas originated and developed into his great masterpieces.

Antonio Forcellino. *The Lost Michelangelos*. Hoboken, NJ: John Wiley & Sons, 2011. Discovery of a *Pietà* may be a rare oil painting by Michelangelo, and restorer and Michelangelo expert Forcellino sets out to prove it. See article below in periodicals.

Andrew Graham-Dixon. *Michelangelo and the Sistine Chapel*. New York: Skyhorse, 2009. A readable, interesting, and perceptive book about the great artist and one of his most famous achievements.

William E. Wallace. *Michelangelo: The Complete Sculpture, Painting, Architecture*. New York: Universe, 2009. A well-written and beautifully illustrated book by a world famous Michelangelo scholar.

Periodicals and Internet Sources

Nicholas Bakalar. "In Vatican Fresco, Visions of the Brain." *New York Times*, June 22, 2010. www.nytimes.com/2010/06/22/science/22brain.html.

Kevin Flynn and Randy Kennedy. "The Pieta Behind the Couch." *New York Times*, May 29, 2011. www.nytimes.com/2011/05/29/arts/design/the-pieta-behind-the-couch.html.

Richard Owen. "'Michelangelo Self-Portrait' Discovered in Restored Vatican Fresco." *Times* (London), July 2, 2009. http://entertainment.timesonline.co.uk/tol/arts_and_entertainment/visual_arts/article6619966.ece.

Elisabetta Povoledo. "Who Owns Michelangelo's *David?*" *New York Times*, August 31, 2010. www.nytimes.com/2010/09/01/world/europe/01david.html.

Robyn Young. "*David:* Anatomy of a Perfect Wreck." *Times* (London), September 8, 2004. www.timesonline.co.uk/tol/news/uk/health/article479938.ece.

Websites

The Digital Michelangelo Project (http://graphics.stanford.edu/projects/mich). Digital scanning of the works of Michelangelo, including essays, videos, and photos.

Michelangelo Buonarroti (www.michelangelo.com/buonarroti.html). Well-done, interesting, and attractive website with gift shop, related links, photos, quotations, and videos.

Michelangelo Buonarroti Quiz (www.surfnetkids.com/games/michelangelo_buonarroti_quiz.htm). A quiz testing readers' knowledge of Michelangelo..

Vatican Museums (http://mv.vatican.va/3_EN/pages/CSN/CSN_Volta.html). Many details about the Sistine Chapel ceiling by Michelangelo.

Videos

The Genius of Michelangelo. DVD video recording by William E. Wallace. Chantilly, VA: The Teaching Company, 2007. Part of "Great Courses" series; includes six discs in three packages with three course guides. For the serious Michelangelo student by a world renowned Michelangelo expert.

Michelangelo Revealed: Secrets of the Dead. DocLab and Compagnie des Taxi Borusse production for Thirteen in association with WNET.org. PBS Home Video, 2009.

Michelangelo: Self-Portrait. Masters and Masterworks Productions. Chicago: Home Vision Entertainment, 2003. This narration and video of Michelangelo's life is told in his own words, using excerpts from his letters and poems.

Index

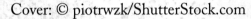

Picture Credits

Cover: © piotrwzk/ShutterStock.com

© Alinari/Art Resource, NY, 81 (left)

© Andrea Jemolo/Scala/Art Resource, NY, 53

© The Art Gallery Collection/Alamy, 10

© Ashmolean Museum/The Art Archive/Art Resource, NY, 93

© Atlantide Phototravel/Corbis, 39

© Bettmann/Corbis, 63

© Conversion of St. Paul (fresco), Buonarroti, Michelangelo (1475-1564)/Cappella Paolina, Vatican, Vatican City/The Bridgeman Art Library, 76

© Corbis, 74

© Erich Lessing/Art Resource, NY, 51, 79

© Foto Marburg/Art Resource, NY, 40

© Gianni Dagli Orti/The Art Archive/Art Resource, NY, 84

© HIP/Art Resource, NY, 24

© imagebroker/Alamy, 45

© Interfoto/Alamy, 87

© James L. Stanfield/National Geographic/Getty Images, 98

© Michael Freeman/Alamy, 35

© Nicolo Orsi Battaglini/Art Resource, NY, 18

© Peter Harrison/Alamy, 13

© Réunion des Musées Nationaux/Art Resource, NY, 56

© Reuters/Corbis, 49

© Scala/Art Resource, NY, 25, 28, 30, 32, 37, 60, 64, 65, 68, 70, 81 (right), 91

© 20th Century Fox/The Kobal Collection/Art Resource, NY, 47

About the Author

Phyllis Raybin Emert is the author of forty-nine books on a wide variety of subjects—from art, animals, and automobiles to unsolved mysteries and women in the Civil War. This is her fourth title for Lucent Books. Her others are *Art in Glass*, *Pottery*, and *Sonia Sotomayor*. Emert lives in New York City with her husband, Larry, and has two grown children, a son-in-law, and one large dog.